PAUL

for

EVERYONE

GALATIANS AND
THESSALONIANS

PAUL
for
EVERYONE

GALATIANS AND THESSALONIANS

TOM WRIGHT

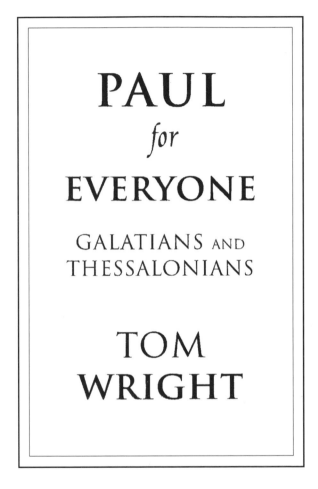

SPCK

Westminster John Knox Press

First published in Great Britain in 2002 by
Society for Promoting Christian Knowledge
Holy Trinity Church
Marylebone Road
London NW1 4DU

This second edition copublished in 2004 by the Society for Promoting
Christian Knowledge, London, and Westminster John Knox Press, 100
Witherspoon Street, Louisville, KY 40202.

04 05 06 07 08 09 10 11 12 13 — 10 9 8 7 6 5 4 3

British Library Cataloguing-in-Publication Data
A catalogue record for this book is available from the British Library.

ISBN: 0-281-05304-9 (U.K. edition)

United States Library of Congress Cataloging-in-Publication Data is
on file at the Library of Congress, Washington, D.C.

ISBN: 0-664-22785-6 (U.S. edition)

Typeset by Pioneer Associates, Perthshire
Printed in Great Britain at
Ashford Colour Press

CONTENTS

CONTENTS

For

Chloe, Sam and David

a small gift from
an often absent Godfather

INTRODUCTION

On the very first occasion when someone stood up in public to tell people about Jesus, he made it very clear: this message is for *everyone*.

It was a great day – sometimes called the birthday of the church. The great wind of God's spirit had swept through Jesus' followers and filled them with a new joy and a sense of God's presence and power. Their leader, Peter, who only a few weeks before had been crying like a baby because he'd lied and cursed and denied even knowing Jesus, found himself on his feet explaining to a huge crowd that something had happened which had changed the world for ever. What God had done for him, Peter, he was beginning to do for the whole world: new life, forgiveness, new hope and power were opening up like spring flowers after a long winter. A new age had begun in which the living God was going to do new things in the world – beginning then and there with the individuals who were listening to him. 'This promise is for *you*,' he said, 'and for your children, and for everyone who is far away' (Acts 2.39). It wasn't just for the person standing next to you. It was for everyone.

Within a remarkably short time this came true to such an extent that the young movement spread throughout much of the known world. And one way in which the *everyone* promise worked out was through the writings of the early Christian leaders. These short works – mostly letters and stories about Jesus – were widely circulated and eagerly read. They were never intended for either a religious or intellectual elite. From the very beginning they were meant for everyone.

That is as true today as it was then. Of course, it matters that some people give time and care to the historical evidence, the meaning of the original words (the early Christians wrote in Greek), and the exact and particular force of what different writers were saying about God, Jesus, the world and themselves. This series is based quite closely on that sort of work. But the point of it all is that the message can get out to everyone, especially to people who wouldn't normally read a book with footnotes and Greek words in it. That's the sort of person for whom these books are written. And that's why there's a glossary, in the back, of the key words that you can't really get along without, with a simple description of what they mean. Whenever you see a word in **bold type** in the text, you can go to the back and remind yourself what's going on.

There are of course many translations of the New Testament available today. The one I offer here is designed for the same kind of reader: one who mightn't necessarily understand the more formal, sometimes even ponderous, tones of some of the standard ones. I have of course tried to keep as close to the original as I can. But my main aim has been to be sure that the words can speak not just to some people, but to everyone.

The three letters in this book were among the first, perhaps the very first, that Paul wrote to the young churches. That means they are the very earliest documents we possess from the beginning of the church's existence. They are already full of life, bubbling with energy, with questions, problems, excitement, danger and, above all, a sense of the presence and power of the living God, who has changed the world through Jesus and is now at work in a new way by his Spirit. So here it is: Paul for everyone – Galatians and Thessalonians!

Tom Wright

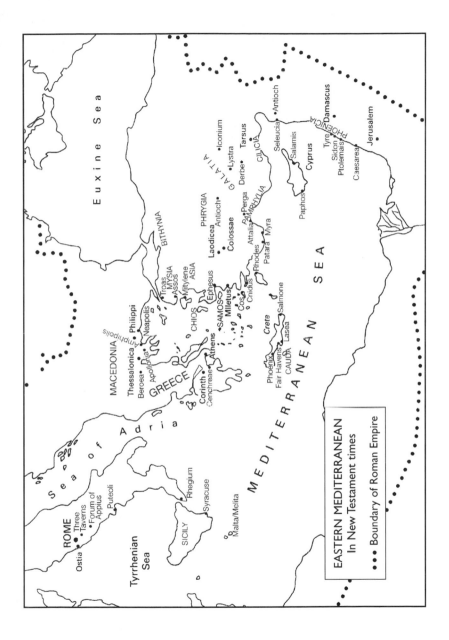

EASTERN MEDITERRANEAN
In New Testament times
••••• Boundary of Roman Empire

GALATIANS

GALATIANS 1.1–9

Paul's Distress Over the Galatians

¹Paul, an apostle ... (my apostleship doesn't derive from human sources! Nor did it come through a human being. It came through Jesus the Messiah, and God the father who raised him from the dead) ... ²and the family who are with me; to the churches of Galatia. ³Grace to you and peace from God our father and Jesus the Messiah, our Lord, ⁴who gave himself for our sins, to rescue us from the present evil age, according to the will of God, our father, ⁵to whom be glory to the ages of ages. Amen.

⁶I'm astonished that you are turning away so quickly from the one who called you by grace, and going after another gospel – ⁷not that it is another gospel, it's just that there are some people stirring up trouble for you and wanting to pervert the gospel of the Messiah. ⁸But even if we – or an angel from heaven! – should announce a gospel other than the one we announced to you, let such a person be accursed. ⁹I said it before and I now say it again: if anyone offers you a gospel other than the one you received, let that person be accursed.

Imagine you're in South Africa in the 1970s. Apartheid is at its height. You are embarked on a risky project: to build a community centre where everybody will be equally welcome, no matter what their colour or race. You've designed it; you've laid the foundation in such a way that only the right sort of building can be built. Or so you think.

You are called away urgently to another part of the country. A little later you get a letter. A new group of builders are building on your foundation. They have changed the design, and are installing two meeting rooms, with two front doors, one for whites only and one for blacks only. Some of the local people are mightily relieved. They always thought there was going to be trouble, putting everyone together like that. Others, though, asked the builders why the original idea wouldn't do.

Oh, said the builders airily, that chap who laid the foundation, he had some funny ideas. He didn't really have permission to make that design. He'd got a bit muddled. We're from the real authorities. This is how it's got to be.

Now imagine you're in central south Turkey during the reign of the Roman Emperor Claudius. Most of the town worship one or other of the local gods or goddesses, several of whom claim the loyalty of particular racial groups. Some have started to worship the emperor himself, and with him the power of Rome. There is also a significant minority of Jews, with their own synagogue. They are threatened by the growing power of the imperial cult, on top of the usual pagan idolatry and wickedness. And into this town has come a funny little Jew called Paul . . .

Paul's project is, he often says, building: but he's building with people, not with bricks and mortar. He lays foundations for this building by telling people some news which is so good it's shocking. According to Paul, there is one God, the world's creator (standard stuff for the Jews, that), and this one God has now unveiled his long-awaited plan for the world. The unveiling took place in a Jew called Jesus; Paul says this Jesus is the Jewish **Messiah**, a kind of king-to-end-all-kings (sounds like a challenge to Emperor Claudius). Jesus was executed by the Romans; that's what they did, often enough, to other people's kings. But Paul says that the true God raised Jesus from the dead.

That's the beginning of the **good news**, but it doesn't stop there. According to Paul, Jesus' death and **resurrection** mean that this God is now building a new family, a single family, a family with no divisions, no separate races, no one-table-for-Jews-and-another-for-**Gentiles** nonsense. Jews believed that when the Messiah came he would be Lord of all the world; so, Paul argues, he'd have to have just one family. And, though this family is the fulfilment of what this God had promised to the Jews, the remarkable thing is that, because of Jesus, you don't have to be a Jew to belong. The God of Israel wants to be known as 'father' by the whole world. So, with this good news, Paul has laid the foundation of a people-building in central south Turkey. Then he has moved on.

And then he hears the bad news. Other people-builders have come in. Oh, they've said, Paul didn't really know what he was doing. You could get into trouble for that kind of thing. In any case, Paul just got his funny ideas by muddling up things that other people had said to him. We've got it from the real authorities. This people-building has to have two sections. Yes, we all believe that Jesus is the Messiah; but we can't have Jewish believers and Gentile believers living as though they were part of the same family. If the Gentile believers want to be part of the real inner circle, the family God promised to Abraham, they will have to become Jews. The men must be **circumcised**. All must keep the **law**, must do the things that keep Jews and Gentiles neatly separated. That's the real good news, they said: you're welcome into God's family if you follow the law of Moses.

Think about that scenario, and you'll see why, in this opening paragraph of his letter to Galatia, Paul sounds as though he's trying to say several things at once, all of them pretty sharp. The key things he's talking about are *apostleship* and *gospel*. Grasp these, and the rest of the letter will start to make sense.

Paul's opponents in Galatia – the rival builders, if you like – had persuaded the Galatians that Paul was only an **apostle** at second hand. The word 'apostle' means 'one who is sent', and came to be a technical term in early Christianity for the original ones whom Jesus sent out after his resurrection. The opponents have suggested that Paul got his apostleship, and the **message** that he announced, from other early Christians, not from Jesus himself. They, by contrast, got theirs (so they claim) from Jerusalem, from the 'original' apostles such as Peter, and James the brother of Jesus.

Not so, replies Paul. His apostleship, his commission to build this new family, came from God himself, and from Jesus the Messiah. Paul's vision of Jesus on the road to Damascus is absolutely central for him and his work.

So too is 'the gospel'. For Paul, this isn't a system of salvation, or a new way of being religious. It's the announcement that Jesus, the crucified Messiah, is exalted as Lord of the whole world; therefore he is calling into existence a single worldwide family. This is the true gospel, he says; beware of illicit imitations. Indeed, shun them; they are a curse, not a blessing.

Paul's apostolic aim to build a single Jesus-based family by announcing this gospel has been partially successful and partially not. It's as much a challenge in our day as it has ever been. In the wider world, ethnic rivalry and hostility continue unabated. Isn't it time for the church to rediscover the apostolic gospel, and to live by it?

GALATIANS 1.10–17

Paul's Conversion and Call

[10]Well now . . . does *that* sound as though I'm trying to make up to people – or to God? Or that I'm trying to curry favour with people? If I were still pleasing people, I wouldn't be a slave of the Messiah.

[11]You see, brothers and sisters, let me make it clear to you: the gospel announced by me is not a mere human invention. [12]I didn't receive it from human beings, nor was I taught it; it came through an unveiling of Jesus the Messiah.

[13]You heard, didn't you, the way I behaved when I was still within 'Judaism'. I persecuted the church of God violently, and ravaged it. [14]I advanced in Judaism beyond many of my fellow-Jewish contemporaries; I was extremely zealous for my ancestral traditions. [15]But when God, who set me apart from my mother's womb, and called me by his grace, was pleased

¹⁶to unveil his son in me, so that I might announce the good news about him among the nations – immediately I did not confer with flesh and blood. ¹⁷Nor did I go up to Jerusalem to those who were apostles before me. No; I went away to Arabia, and afterwards returned to Damascus.

John Henry Newman was one of the great figures of nineteenth-century England. A brilliant thinker and writer, a spellbinding preacher and a deeply sensitive soul, he left the Anglican Church and became a Roman Catholic in 1845. After a long career in which his friends, at least, wondered what had become of the early brilliance, he was made a cardinal.

Many English Protestants could never forgive Newman for what they saw as his treachery. One in particular, the clergyman and novelist Charles Kingsley, accused Newman of what today we would call double-think, of sitting light to truth. Newman, goaded beyond endurance, produced as his answer one of the century's classics, his *Apologia pro Vita Sua* (1864). He went back to the beginning and told his own story up to and beyond his move to Rome. The depth and transparency of the story carried its own weight. Even those who did not agree with the positions Newman adopted could hardly doubt that they were reached sincerely and out of a passion for, not a disregard of, truth itself.

Paul was in a somewhat similar position. His opponents had been saying that he had tailored his **gospel** to please people. Presumably they imagined Paul's failure to have **Gentile** converts **circumcised** was just a trick to please people, giving them the gospel on the cheap. Most of us like to be liked; many, in pursuit of this goal, are prepared to say what they think people want to hear.

The opening nine verses of the letter make it quite clear that this wasn't how Paul operated. Verse 10, in fact, implies that they were designed to make exactly this impression. They were deliberately written, it seems, so that Paul could then pause for breath and say, with a wry smile, 'So, you thought I was looking for human approval, did you?' Like Shakespeare's Demetrius in *A Midsummer Night's Dream*, Paul says to himself, 'Well roar'd, lion.' He can now adopt a somewhat gentler tone: 'So, can I make it any plainer to you that I am not seeking human approval, writing stuff like that?' No, he says, that's not my business. I'm the **Messiah**'s slave; that's all that matters.

He then sets about telling how he came by his gospel, and what it did to him when it arrived. Like Newman telling his story to silence his critics, Paul explains where he had come from, how he had been confronted with the revelation of the risen Jesus, and what immediate effects all this had had.

Paul grew up with definite role models. Long before football stars and rock musicians, Jewish boys like Paul had their minds fed with tales of the Jewish heroes of long ago, the prophets and martyrs who had lived and died fearlessly for their God and his **law**. Paul describes himself as one of those who were strictest and keenest in their adherence to, and their application of, the ancestral traditions, that is, the detailed discussions as to how precisely the law of Moses should be applied in day-to-day living. He was, in other words, a **Pharisee**, and a strict one at that. We know what sort of role models someone like that would have. The chief one was the prophet Elijah.

Elijah was a man of fire. He called down fire on soldiers sent to seize him. He called down fire on the prophets of Baal. He was feared by all who sought to compromise their obedience to the one God of Israel by worshipping idols. Just the man for a young Pharisee like Saul of Tarsus to emulate. And he did. He ravaged the church, just as (alas) some try to do today, not least in parts of Africa and Asia. He saw himself, it seems, as a latter-day Elijah, cleansing Israel of the horrible nonsense about Jesus of Nazareth, who couldn't have been the Messiah because he was crucified, and who certainly couldn't be worshipped because in any case the Messiah wouldn't be divine.

But then – and here he slips into talking about himself as an Old Testament prophet – Paul was stopped in his tracks, just as Elijah had been. Elijah, dejected and depressed, went off to Mount Sinai to meet his God afresh, to learn about the still small voice as well as the earthquake, wind and fire. Saul of Tarsus went off, probably to Sinai (he says 'Arabia', which is where Sinai was), most likely for a similar private wrestling with the God whom he worshipped. This God, to Saul's horror and amazement, had now revealed his son, and had done so in order that he, Saul, an ultra-orthodox Jew, might tell the pagan nations that Israel's God loved them just as much as he loved Israel.

Where did Paul learn his sense of irony from? Might it not have been from God himself?

We are all different, and as the old Puritans said, God does not break all hearts in the same way. But it is a central strand of most Christian living that everybody needs, from time to time, to wrestle privately with God and his will. It is necessary, too, that Christian leaders should be seen to be telling their own story truly. For Paul, his story was closely linked with God's unveiling of Jesus as the true Messiah, the crucified and risen Lord of the world. His life, his vocation, his whole identity was stamped with the gospel **message**. He was a true **apostle**.

GALATIANS 1.18–24

Paul's First Visit to Peter

[18]Then, after three years, I went up to Jerusalem to speak with Cephas. I stayed with him for two weeks. [19]I didn't see any other of the apostles except James, the Lord's brother [20](what I'm writing to you, see here – in the presence of God, I'm not

telling a lie!). [21]Then I went to the regions of Syria and Cilicia. [22]I remained unknown by sight to the messianic assemblies in Judaea. [23]They simply heard that the one who had been persecuting them was now announcing the good news of the faith which he once tried to destroy. [24]And they glorified God because of me.

A few years ago in England a strange advertisement appeared on large billboards. Without explanation, it simply said, 'IT IS. ARE YOU?'

It was, of course, designed to tease, so that when the answer was revealed a few weeks later everyone had been thinking about it. It was, in fact, a brand new newspaper: the *Independent*. At the time the advertisement felt like a cheap stunt; but it obviously worked, because I can remember it several years later, and the newspaper continues to flourish. It has become, remarkably, a fourth alongside the previous 'big three', *The Times*, the *Telegraph*, and the *Guardian*. Whether it ever was, or is now, actually independent of the different parties and pressure groups in British public life, I am not qualified to say. But there was something magic, something fresh, about the idea of a new voice appearing in the public arena, a voice which wasn't simply going to say what other people, the same boring old power-brokers, had told it to say. We may guess that the other three found it, to say the least, a threat. Whose readers was it stealing?

We could summarize what Paul is saying in this paragraph as: 'I AM. ARE YOU?' The trouble-makers in Galatia have been putting it about that he's simply a pawn of the Judaea Christians, especially the **apostles**. They have suggested that he's just a junior member of the Christian team of wandering preachers. What's more, he's not even a very reliable one! He's twisted the message he was given by the 'senior' apostles, distorting it to make it easier for non-Jews to swallow. So (these trouble-makers have said) listen to us instead. We're the ones who know what the Judaea apostles, the senior folk, the people who actually knew Jesus himself, are thinking. Take it from us.

Paul replies with a detailed description of his first visit to Jerusalem following his conversion. The point of the whole story is to declare the one word: INDEPENDENT. He didn't go and sit at the feet of Peter, James and John, the Big Three of the Judaea apostles. He didn't train under their leadership, or work alongside them in the little churches. He talked to Peter (he uses his Aramaic name, Cephas, which like the Greek word 'Peter' means 'rock'), and indeed stayed with him for a fortnight. He met James the brother of the Lord, who as we know from elsewhere was on his way at this stage to becoming the central leader in the whole Christian movement, even though he hadn't been a believer during Jesus' own lifetime. And that was it. He wasn't their **disciple**. They hadn't commissioned him to be a sub-apostle under their leadership. He was . . . independent.

The point of all this for the Galatian Christians, who had first heard the **good news** of Jesus from Paul's lips, now becomes clear. 'PAUL IS. ARE THEY?' Are they independent of the Judaea apostles? Are they independent even of Paul?

Paul is of course treading a fine line here. He believes that his announcement of the **gospel**, which creates a single family composed of Jews and **Gentiles** together in the **Messiah**, is loyal to Jesus himself. To that extent, he wants them to be loyal to him. But if push comes to shove they must choose the gospel even over him (as he said in 1.8).

Nevertheless, unlike rival newspapers, which will sometimes take a different line just for the sake of being different, Paul has no long-term interest in maintaining that what he says, and what the Jerusalem apostles say, are actually two different messages. The unity of the church matters to him very deeply; ironically, the only way he can work for it in Galatia is to affirm his independence. What he will go on to suggest is that the trouble-makers who have come to Galatia, claiming authority from Jerusalem, are the ones who have got things muddled up. What he, Paul, was preaching as an independent apostle was in fact the same basic message that the Judaean churches were living by.

The end of the paragraph is very telling on this point. The little messianic assemblies in Judaea – on their way to being what we would call 'churches', but at the moment simply synagogues whose members had all become Christians – had never met Paul. But what they heard about him, as he was starting his missionary work in Syria and Cilicia, away to the north where Paul was born, was not 'some wretched fellow is preaching a watered-down, distorted version of the gospel', but rather, 'the man we heard of as a great persecutor is preaching the **faith** he once tried to destroy'. An independent apostle but with the same message. That's the point. So 'they glorified God because of me', or, literally, 'in me'. They didn't grumble to God about this man who was perverting the good news. 'They saw that God was at work in me, the God they knew and loved in Jesus the Messiah and by the **spirit**; and they praised God for this work.'

Centuries have passed. But the issue of the independence and yet convergence of the churches, their teachers, and their gospel is as important now as ever it was. Tragically, we still have 'turf wars' between churches, reflecting all too clearly the racial or cultural tensions of their world; think of the Balkans, or Northern Ireland. We still have people who try to claim that they, or their system, possess supreme authority, and that anyone who professes independence should come back into line. And, ironically, those churches who boast most loudly of their independence are often quickest to set up new and rigid structures of authority.

It is some comfort to know that these problems were endemic in Christianity from the beginning. But it is more important still, in recognizing the problem, to know how to go about tackling it. If Paul is to be our guide, the first rule seems to be: tell the story clearly. Don't fudge the background out of which the problem has come. Learn to prize both the independence which grows out of a fresh vision of Jesus, and the convergence between different preachings of the gospel. But keep your eye on the main issue, which must always be God's glory.

These are only ground rules, not detailed guidelines. But they mattered in the first century and they matter today.

GALATIANS 2.1–5

Standing Firm Against Opposition

¹Then, after fourteen years, I went up again to Jerusalem. I took Barnabas with me, and Titus. ²I went up because of a revelation. I laid before them the gospel which I announce among the Gentiles (I did this privately, in the presence of the key people), in case somehow I might be running, or might have run, to no good effect. ³But even the Greek, Titus, who was with me, was not forced to get circumcised . . . ⁴but because of some pseudo-family members who had been secretly smuggled in, who came in on the side to spy on the freedom which we have in the Messiah, Jesus, so that they might bring us into slavery; ⁵and I didn't yield authority to them, no, not for a moment, so that the truth of the gospel might be maintained for you.

The anthropologist Nigel Barley wrote two famous (and often very funny) books, *The Innocent Anthropologist* and *A Plague of Caterpillars*, about the Dowayo tribe, with whom he lived for a while in a remote part of the African republic of Chad. He learnt their language, complete with all kinds of subtle changes in voice level which could alter a perfectly civil comment into an extremely rude one. He studied their customs and tried to make sense of them: their crop-growing and harvesting, their rain-making rituals, their marriage rules, their respect for, and often fear of, their ancestors. And it gradually became clear to him that the ceremony at the heart of the culture, which made sense of virtually everything else, was the ritual of male **circumcision**.

He never witnessed the ceremony. It was shrouded in secrecy; he could never discover exactly when it was to take place, and it never coincided with his visits. But the question of which boys were circumcised and which ones hadn't yet been (the ritual was carried out at puberty), and of who had been circumcised in company with whom, lay just below the surface in one discussion after another, even when they seemed to be quite unrelated to the ritual itself. Circumcision provided a key badge of identity for the males in the tribe.

Social psychologists can and do come up with theories as to why circumcision plays such a large role in certain cultures. The ritual seems to highlight both the importance of the reproductive function and the fact that sexual appetite is a force that must somehow be controlled (though from Barley's accounts of Dowayo life this aspect is decidedly more symbolic than actual). Its origins are lost in the mists of time, though the Bible speaks of one occasion on which God commanded Abraham that he and his household should be circumcised, as a sign of the **covenant** God had made with Abraham and his family (Genesis 17). The Jews were by no means the only people in the ancient world to wear this badge, just as they are not alone in this respect today.

A good deal of Galatians hinges on the fact that circumcision was the key issue, almost to the point of obsession, in the churches where **Gentiles** had become members, including of course the churches founded by Paul himself. It was all a question of identity, of knowing not only who you were yourself but who else belonged in your group, your tribe, your ethnic family. It didn't matter in the very early church, because all the first Christians were Jews, so all the males were circumcised anyway. But as soon as non-Jews heard the **good news** of Jesus, believed it and got baptized, the question of group identity-markers surfaced, and surfaced quite violently.

In a sense, as we shall see, the problem was about the Jewish **law**. Jews had to keep the law of Moses; surely Christians, believing in the Jewish **Messiah**, would do so as well? Yes and no, says Paul. The Jewish law defines Jews as a family over against all other racial groups, and if people from those groups become Christians they do so on equal terms. This is what Paul will argue at length, from various angles, throughout the rest of this letter.

But the problem focused itself on circumcision for one reason in particular. It was often difficult to tell who precisely was keeping the law of Moses and who wasn't. You couldn't be sure if they were only eating kosher food; you couldn't observe exactly how they kept the **sabbath**. And in any case there were long-running disputes as to what precisely counted in those areas. But with circumcision you knew where you were. A male was either circumcised or he wasn't. A man could no more be partly circumcised than a woman could be partly pregnant. It was a sure-fire test.

That's why Paul, telling the story of his second visit to Jerusalem after his conversion, struggles with the question of Titus and his circumcision. The writing here is jerky and difficult, and perhaps reflects Paul's anger and frustration at the allegations against him.

What seems to have happened is this. The troublemakers in Galatia, doing their best to cast doubt on Paul's apostleship and the completeness of the **gospel** he had preached, had told the Galatian Christians that Paul did after all want non-Jewish Christians to get circumcised. This was a bit of the **message** (they might have said) which he hadn't told them in Galatia, either because he hadn't had time or because he was nervous that it would put them off. After all, they had said, when Paul took Titus to Jerusalem he circumcised him so that Titus could enjoy true fellowship with the Jewish **apostles** there.

This accusation compels Paul to explain what had and hadn't happened. Unfortunately verses 3–5 aren't as clear as we would like, and some people still think that Paul had in fact circumcised Titus even though he doesn't want to admit the fact. (This is after all what, according to Acts 16.3, Paul did to Timothy, so that Timothy could accompany him when preaching in synagogues.) I think it is more likely that Titus wasn't circumcised, and that Paul is simply embarrassed and angry that the issue has been raised at all.

The passage is then affirming three things about Paul's second visit to Jerusalem after his conversion.

First, he didn't go there in order to learn the gospel; he already knew it. He went because God told him to, perhaps through a prophetic 'revelation' (see Acts 11.27–30).

Second, he explained to the Jerusalem apostles what it was that he was preaching in the Gentile world, not in order to learn something new but in order to maintain his unity with what was still the heartland of Christian **faith**.

Third, there had been what he calls some 'false family members', a phrase which he perhaps means as a contemptuous reversal of what they themselves had been saying about Titus. They were, he says, smuggled in to see what this part of the movement looked like, to see who these people were who claimed to follow Jesus but who didn't bother about keeping the law of Moses. Yes, there were some such, says Paul; but I didn't give way to them for a moment. What was and is at stake is 'the truth of the gospel'.

Why? Because the gospel is the announcement that the crucified and risen Jesus is Lord of the world. And if he is Lord of the whole world, then those who believe in him, who give allegiance to him, must form a single family. There cannot be divisions based on nationhood or race. If the church had learnt this from Paul, instead of conveniently forgetting it, many troubles in today's world might have been averted.

What about tomorrow? Will the church now learn the lesson? Will it demonstrate it before the watching world?

GALATIANS 2.6–10

Paul's Agreement with Peter and James

⁶However, those who had the reputation of being Something – what sort of 'thing' they were makes no difference to me, God shows no partiality – those of reputation added nothing extra to me. ⁷On the contrary, they saw that I had been entrusted with the gospel for the uncircumcision, just as Peter had been with the gospel for the circumcision ⁸(for the one who gave Peter the power to be an apostle to the circumcision gave me the power to go to the Gentiles). They knew, moreover, the grace that had been given to me. ⁹So James, Cephas and John, who were reputed to be 'pillars', gave to Barnabas and me the right hand of fellowship, that we should go to the Gentiles, and they to the circumcision. ¹⁰The only extra thing they asked was that we should continue to remember the poor – the very thing I was eager to do.

One of the most famous walks in England is along a high ridge in the Lake District called Striding Edge. It runs to the east of the mountain called Helvellyn, one of the highest mountains in England, and, particularly in bad weather, one of the most dangerous. Most English mountains are relatively safe, but that's one of the ones that isn't. I've climbed Helvellyn a number of times, including in thick snow, but I've never walked Striding Edge, and I now wonder if I'm getting too old for it.

The difficulty about Striding Edge, as you can tell from pictures and from what past hikers have written, is that it's so narrow and high. At many points you can look down past your right foot into one valley, a thousand feet below, and past your left foot into another, equally far below. A cool head and a steady nerve are what's needed up there. And the path – well, the path naturally jerks and jogs its way along, twisting this way and that, keeping to the top of the ridge because that's the only way forward. A pace to the right or the left – or a pace straight ahead when the ridge twists to right or left – and you'll be over the edge.

Paul is walking along a real Striding Edge in this argument, and that's why his writing twists and turns this way and that. Down past his right foot he can see a sheer drop over one cliff: if he stresses too much the fact that James, Peter and John approved of his preaching the **gospel** to the **Gentiles**, his opponents will say 'There you are! We told you! He just got it from them and now he's muddled it up, as we said!' But at the same time, down past his left foot, he can see the sheer drop over another cliff: if he labours the point that God doesn't care who's who in the church, that all are equal in his sight, and that the Jerusalem **apostles** are ultimately no more important than anyone else, he runs the risk of breaking fellowship with the centre of Christian **faith**. And for Paul the unity of the church is absolutely vital. Unity is the summit of the mountain, the goal at the other end of the dangerous ridge, and because Paul is determined to get there in one piece he keeps to the path, even though it means sudden jerky changes of direction.

Three times he speaks of those who 'seemed', or had the 'reputation', of being something special. Paul was of course sensitive about this; the Jerusalem apostles had been following Jesus from the beginning, and the only one who hadn't was Jesus' own brother. They had a kind of natural seniority which he couldn't match. The first two times he mentions their reputation, in verse 6, he takes a sharp step to the left: who they may or may not have been makes no difference to me, because God is no respecter of persons. God doesn't care whether someone has blue or brown eyes, is old or young, tall or short, fat or thin, male or female, rich or poor, well known or unknown. God's love for all alike is part of the gospel; forget it for a moment and you're over the cliff.

The third time he mentions it, in verse 9, he gives these 'special' people their nickname, which has passed into popular English speech in a more general sense. They were, he says, known as the 'pillars' (we speak of someone being 'a pillar of the community'). Pillars are normally used only for very grand buildings; and the most obvious such building in Jerusalem was of course the **Temple**. James, Peter and John were known as the 'pillars' because, we must assume, the early church saw itself in some sense as the new Temple.

Three times he describes what happened at his meeting with these 'pillars'. First, they added nothing to him. They didn't tell him his gospel was deficient, that he should add the command to get circumcised. Second, they were happy to agree a division of labour: he would go to the Gentile world, and they to the Jewish world. (That seems to give Paul a lot more territory; it reminds me of those old letter-boxes in London which had two slots, one labelled LONDON and the other one ALL OTHER PLACES. But there were Jews all over the Mediterranean world by this stage, so Peter's field was not exactly small, either.) Third, they urged him to go on remembering the poor. The reason Paul and Barnabas were in Jerusalem at this moment was almost certainly to bring financial aid to the churches there who were suffering from famine (see Acts 11.27–30).

Paul has successfully negotiated the ridge. He has made it clear that he wasn't in the pocket of the Jerusalem apostles. But he has also made it clear that they were very happy about him and his work.

Underneath it all, as the guiding hand to help Paul keep his balance, was the secret but vital work of God. 'The one who energized Peter and me . . .' is a way of speaking about the strange, intimate and powerful work of the one God. 'They knew', he says, 'the grace that had been given me.' If only church leaders, and ordinary members, could be humble enough to recognize the gracious work of the one God in and through those who work in a different way, with different people, and with different traditions, the gospel would go forward no matter how steep the cliff on either side.

GALATIANS 2.11–14

Paul Confronts Peter in Antioch

[11]But when Cephas came to Antioch, I stood up to him. He was in the wrong. [12]Before certain persons came from James, Peter was eating with the Gentiles. But when they came, he drew back and separated himself, because he was afraid of the circumcision-people. [13]The rest of the Jews did the same, joining him in this play-acting. Even Barnabas was carried along by their sham. [14]But when I saw that they weren't walking straight down the line of gospel truth, I said to Cephas in front of them all: 'Look here: you're a Jew, but you've been living like a Gentile. How can you force Gentiles to become Jews?'

When my brother was at school, he took part in a performance of 'Noye's Fludde' by Benjamin Britten. Actually, he took the part of Noah himself. His costume and make-up were superb. Though he was only 17, he looked like a really old man, complete with beard and grey hair. The production required him to make an entrance through the main door of the auditorium; but, when he got there, an overzealous usher, failing to recognize him, took him for an elderly down-and-out and tried to stop him getting in. It was a great compliment to the make-up artist.

In the ancient Greek theatre make-up wasn't quite so advanced, so they had a standard technique to help the audience suspend their disbelief. Actors had masks, which they held in front of their faces on the end of a stick. The obvious deception took nobody in, but it enabled the spectators to enter into the drama more thoroughly. The Greek word for 'play-acting', referring to people who were pretending to be something when they were in fact something else, is the word from which we get our words *hypocrite* and *hypocrisy*. Already by Paul's day these words didn't just mean 'actor'. They meant what our words mean, someone deceitfully playing a part, pretending to be something they aren't.

This is the charge Paul levelled at Peter in their famous confrontation at Antioch. (Antioch, near the north-eastern corner of the Mediterranean, about 300 miles away from Jerusalem, was one of the great centres of early Christianity; according to Acts 11.26, this was the first place where the followers of Jesus were called 'Christians', '**Messiah**-people'.) Paul was one of the young leaders in the church in Antioch, and there it had clearly been the custom that Jewish Christians and **Gentile** Christians would eat together at the same table.

It's hard for Westerners today to see how serious a matter table-fellowship was in the early church. We are accustomed to sitting down in a café – in a railway station, for instance – and sharing a table with anyone who happens to be there. Granted, if we go to a restaurant we expect to have a table for ourselves and our party. But if we're eating, say, with colleagues from work, we don't stop to enquire about their ethnic background. A moment's thought, however, will remind us that there have been many places in the world until very recently, and that there still are some, where if your skin is the wrong colour, or if you are known to belong to the wrong religion, or perhaps simply if your accent gives you away as the wrong sort of person, there will be some who will not sit down and eat with you. There are even, in some places, laws that forbid such mixing. Eating with people is one of the most powerful symbols of association. Just as **circumcision** is a symbol which speaks of family identity, so is table-fellowship.

The question of Peter's play-acting, therefore, first in his eating with non-Jewish Christians and then in his refusal to do so, is intimately related to the question in the previous paragraph, whether Gentile Christians had to be circumcised in order to belong to God's people. It's all part of the same issue, the issue that was urgently at stake in Galatia itself.

So why is Paul telling them about this confrontation in Antioch, and why does he say Peter and Barnabas were play-acting?

It is likely that the troublemakers in Galatia had already told the new converts there that Paul and Peter had had an argument in Antioch over whether Gentile Christians were really full members of the family. They may have heard a version of the story in which Peter had the strongest arguments; and the story, told this way, was powerful reinforcement for their own case to the puzzled Galatians. 'There, you see,' they would say; 'Paul hadn't told you the whole story. Peter was after all Jesus' right-hand man. He knew that you couldn't belong to the true Israel without becoming a full Jew. He drew the line at table-fellowship with uncircumcised Gentiles.'

So Paul has to tell the story his way, to bring out the fact that this wasn't just a squabble between two ways of interpreting one comparatively trivial point; it involved the very heart of the **gospel**. (One of the most vital aspects of Christian leadership is the ability to discern the issues that really matter, and to explain why.) He distinguishes between the real Peter and the play-acting Peter, the Peter holding a mask in front of his face and pretending to be someone else.

The real Peter is the Peter who knows in his bones that, in Jesus the Messiah, God has created one new family of Jews and Gentiles alike. It's hard to live like that after a lifetime of looking at Gentiles as almost a different species; but Peter has been doing it. Then, just as when Peter walked on the water but looked down at the waves around his feet, something happened which caused him to sink. Certain persons arrived from James. Paul doesn't say that James had sent them; but

Peter knew they were hard-liners, who wouldn't approve of the Antioch practice. So he holds the mask of Jewish respectability in front of his real face, which means that for the moment he will separate himself from the Gentile Christians. So convincing is his mask that the other Jewish Christians are taken in by it, like the usher on the auditorium door. And even Barnabas (we can feel Paul's sorrow and anger concentrated in that word 'even'; Barnabas had been his close friend and colleague) goes along with the play-acting, the mask-wearing, the sham.

Paul's confrontation is direct and to the point. 'Peter, you've been living like a Gentile, making no distinction between Jews and non-Jews. How can you now insist, as your behaviour is insisting, on Gentiles becoming Jews in order to become part of the inner circle of God's people?'

So far, the charge is simple inconsistency. Peter has been doing one thing one minute and the opposite the next. Paul is about to go on to develop the point with more theological scaffolding. But his fundamental point, which echoes down the centuries of church history as a warning to all who want to put on masks of respectability from time to time, is quite clear. All those in Christ must be who they truly are. You don't need masks or make-up in the **kingdom of God**.

GALATIANS 2.15–21

Justified by Faith, Not Works of Law

[15]We are Jews by birth, not 'Gentile sinners'. [16]But we know that a person is not declared 'righteous' by works of the Jewish law, but through the faithfulness of Jesus the Messiah.

That is why we too believed in the Messiah, Jesus: so that we might be declared 'righteous' on the basis of the Messiah's faithfulness, and not on the basis of works of the Jewish law. On that basis, you see, no creature will be declared 'righteous'.

[17]Well, then; if, in seeking to be declared 'righteous' in the

Messiah, we ourselves are found to be 'sinners', does that make the Messiah an agent of 'sin'? Certainly not! [18]If I build up once more the things which I tore down, I demonstrate that I am a lawbreaker.

[19]Let me explain it like this. Through the law I died to the law, so that I might live to God. [20]I have been crucified with the Messiah. I am, however, alive – but it isn't me, it's the Messiah who lives in me. And the life I do still live in the flesh, I live within the faithfulness of the son of God, who loved me and gave himself for me.

[21]I don't set aside God's grace. If 'righteousness' comes through the law, then the Messiah died for nothing.

A well-known story is told of Margaret Thatcher during the time she was Prime Minister of the United Kingdom. She was visiting an old people's home, going from room to room and meeting senior citizens who had lived there a long time. One old lady showed no sign of realizing that she was shaking hands with a world-famous politician. 'Do you know who I am?' asked Mrs Thatcher. 'No, dear,' replied the old lady, 'but I should ask the nurse if I were you. She usually knows.'

It is a strange idea to most of us, but for some a very necessary one: that you might begin again from scratch *to learn who you are*. That is precisely what people who have suffered severe memory loss need to do. It is what people who have suffered other kinds of loss also need to do: the refugee without home, country or family is but one example. And it's precisely this sort of exercise, losing one identity and reconstructing another, that Paul is explaining in this dense and complex passage.

This is where he really gets to grips with the underlying issues between himself and the 'troublemakers'. It isn't a matter of a few twists and turns in the interpretation of the **gospel**, or for that matter of the Jewish **law**. It isn't simply about one style of missionary policy as against another. It is a matter of *who you are in the* **Messiah**. It's as basic as that. Paul's head-on clash with Peter in Antioch was about Christian identity. His passionate appeal to the Galatians is about their Christian identity.

Often Paul's dense paragraphs, like this one, yield their secrets if you approach them from near the end, where he sums everything up in a single great climactic statement. In this case it is verses 19b–20: 'I have been crucified with the Messiah! – I am alive, however, but it isn't me; it's the Messiah, living in me! And what about the life I continue to live in this mortal flesh? Well, that is lived by the faithfulness of the son of God, who loved me and gave himself for me.' This is the heart of Paul's argument. One must lose everything, including the memory of who one was before; and one must accept, and learn to live by, a new identity, with a new foundation.

The question Paul and Peter have run into, which was focused on whether Jewish and **Gentile** Christians were allowed to eat at the same table, is the question: who is God's true Israel? Who are the true people of God? Is it all who belong to the Messiah? Or is it only Jewish Christians (including proselytes, i.e., Gentiles who have converted to Judaism), with Gentile Christians remaining second-class citizens?

Paul focuses his answer on the most basic point of all. God's true Israel consists of one person: the Messiah. He is the faithful one. He is the true Israelite. This is the foundation of identity within God's people.

The question then becomes: who *belongs* to the Messiah? How is *that* identity expressed?

Paul answers this with one of his most famous beliefs, which remains difficult for modern Western minds to come to terms with. Those who belong to the Messiah are *in the Messiah*, so that what is true of him is true of them. The roots of this idea are in the Jewish beliefs about the king. The king represents his people (think of David fighting Goliath, *representing* Israel against the Philistines); what is true of him is true of them. The present paragraph doesn't spell this out; it assumes it. Paul will return to it in more detail later on. His point here is quite simple: all who are 'in the Messiah' are the true people of God. *And that means Gentiles as well as Jews.*

He speaks of himself, as a Jew who had become a Christian, to make the point. We Jews, he says, even though we were born into the **covenant** family, do not now find our real identity as God's people through the things which mark us out as a distinctive people – that is, through the Jewish law. If we believe that Jesus is the Messiah (and without that there is no Christianity), we believe that the *crucified* Jesus is the Messiah. And if we are 'in' the crucified Jesus, that means that our previous identities are irrelevant. They are to be forgotten. We are no longer defined by possession of the law, or by its detailed requirements that set Jew over against Gentile. 'I died to the law, that I might live to God.' We must now learn who we are in a whole new way.

Who then are we? We are the Messiah's people, with his life now at work in us. And, since the central thing about him is his loving faithfulness, the central thing about us, the only thing in fact that defines us, is our own loving faithfulness, the glad response of **faith** to the God who has sent his son to die for us. This is the very heart of Christian identity.

The words Paul uses as his shorthand for Christian identity, for belonging to God's family, are usually translated 'righteous' and 'righteousness'. This English word has different meanings to different people. For Paul, as we shall see in the next chapter, it is related to God's promise to Abraham, now fulfilled in the Messiah, that God would create a single worldwide family, whose identity-marker would be faith. And it speaks of the family identity, the status of covenant membership, which God gives to all his family, to all who believe the gospel. Out beyond that, it speaks gloriously of God's saving justice embracing and healing the whole unjust world, and rescuing in the present those men, women and children who trust his love revealed in Jesus. This is the people who are 'declared righteous', or 'justified'.

The point of it all, here in Galatians, is quite simple. Paul was demonstrating to Peter that even Jewish Christians have lost their old identity, defined by the law, and have come into a new identity, defined only by the Messiah.

This doesn't mean, as he says in verses 17–18, that by losing Jewish identity we are 'sinners', as the Jews had regarded the Gentiles. On the contrary, if like Peter you reconstruct the wall between Jews and Gentiles, all you achieve is to prove that you yourself are a lawbreaker. If the law is what really matters, then look out: you've broken it!

But the law isn't now the thing that matters. 'If righteousness (covenant membership, **justification**) came by the Jewish **law**, then the Messiah wouldn't have needed to die.' To have separate tables within the church is to spurn the generous love of the Messiah. One of the marks of Jesus' public career was open table-fellowship. God intends it to be a mark of Jesus' people from that day to this.

GALATIANS 3.1–9

God's Promise and Abraham's Faith

[1]You witless Galatians! Who has bewitched you? King Jesus was portrayed on the cross before your very eyes! [2]There's just one thing I want to know from you. Did you receive the spirit by doing the works of Torah – or by hearing and believing? [3]You are so witless: you began with the spirit, and now you're ending with the flesh? [4]Did you really suffer so much for nothing – if indeed it is going to be for nothing? [5]The one who gives you the spirit and performs powerful deeds among you – does he do this through your performance of Torah, or through hearing and believing?

[6]It's like Abraham. 'He believed God, and it was counted to him for righteousness.' [7]So you know that it's people of faith who are children of Abraham. [8]The Bible foresaw that God would justify the nations by faith, so it announced the gospel to Abraham in advance, when it declared that 'the nations will

be blessed in you'. [9]So you see: the people of faith are blessed along with faithful Abraham.

A famous story tells of the tight-rope walker Charles Blondin (1824–97), who set up a rope across Niagara Falls and walked across several times. So confident did he become that he made the journey backwards as well as forwards, and performed various tricks on the way, like sitting on a small stool and eating a meal. But the most famous trick was when he asked for a volunteer to be carried over on his back. In what must be one of the most supreme acts of physical trust ever placed by one human being in another, a brave, or perhaps foolish, man stepped forward, and was carried over on the great man's shoulders.

Now supposing, halfway across, the man had said to Blondin: 'Look here, this is all very well, but I really don't trust you any more. I think I'd better do the rest by myself. Let me down and I'll walk from here without you.' One can only imagine the retort he would have got, not only from the professional, but from any watching friends or family. Had he taken leave of his senses? How did he suppose he would get across by himself?

That is exactly the reaction Paul has on hearing that his beloved Galatians are thinking of getting **circumcised**. Who has cast a spell on them? Are they out of their minds? Twice he calls them 'mindless' or 'witless'; they seem to have lost the power to think straight. Having begun in the **spirit**, do they think they can continue in the flesh? Having begun with **faith**, do they think they can continue with works of the Jewish **law**, the **Torah**?

To understand why this is so obviously nonsense to Paul, we need to remind ourselves what was at stake. He was concerned above all about who the Galatians thought they were. Were they part of the **Messiah**-family, the people who belonged to the new age which had begun with Jesus' death and **resurrection**?

Or were they trying to become part of the physical family of Israel, joining, by circumcision, the people of God defined by ethnic origin? Paul repeats in the first verse the point made at the end of chapter 2: once Jesus the Messiah had been portrayed before them as crucified, how could they ever think that membership in the physical family of Israel was an option? (The word 'portrayed' may mean that he actually drew a large picture of a cross, to show them what had happened to Jesus. I was once asked by a tourist in a train to tell him about Jesus, and had to do the same thing. However, most people in the ancient world knew only too well what crosses did, and what they looked like, and it's possible that Paul just means that he described Jesus' crucifixion very vividly.)

He gives them in this passage two very solid initial reasons why they shouldn't get off and try to walk by themselves. First, God has given them his spirit; second, they are already the true children of Abraham. This is the first time he has mentioned either, and both are going to be very important as the letter proceeds.

For Paul the spirit (we might write 'Spirit', but Paul shifts easily to and fro between God's spirit and the human spirit, and it's easier to keep the same form) was God's own spirit, powerfully active wherever the **good news** of Jesus was announced. It was because the spirit was at work in Paul's preaching that the Galatians came to believe in the first place, as Paul says in 1 Thessalonians 1.5. Paul can talk about the 'word' of God, when preached, as itself active (1 Thessalonians 2.13), or about the **gospel** itself as carrying this power (Romans 1.16); or he can declare that it is only by the spirit that one can make the most basic confession of Christian faith, that 'Jesus is Lord' (1 Corinthians 12.3). Putting these together, the point is that when the word of the gospel is preached the spirit of God works in people's hearts to bring them to faith.

Now, Paul says, if you get circumcised you are saying that it isn't the spirit that matters but the flesh – the flesh of your foreskins, and 'the flesh' as the whole sphere of existence of humanity in rebellion against God. You are climbing off the back of the one who is carrying you to safety, and insisting on doing things in the way that you know will lead to disaster. You are forgetting how this whole thing started, and thinking you can reinvent the rules halfway across. You are ignoring the fact that all you presently enjoy – the present spiritual life of the church, and the powerful things God does in your midst, works of healing and the like – happen because of the spirit, and happen in the context of your trust in God's grace. The Galatians didn't become Christians through keeping the Jewish law, which deals with the things of the flesh; they don't continue as Christians by observing the Jewish law. Being a Christian starts and continues as a matter of faith. The Jewish law has nothing to say to it.

Paul has thus lined up 'spirit' and 'faith' on the one hand, and 'flesh' and 'law' on the other. This double either/or will be important as the letter proceeds. But now he turns to the central theme of the letter: if you believe the gospel, you are already a child of Abraham in every sense that matters.

It's possible that the 'agitators' had been insisting to the Galatians that to be true children of Abraham – and hence true Israelites, true monotheists, truly on the road to salvation – they needed to keep the Jewish law and therefore get circumcised. But, though Paul may be answering an argument like that, there is no doubt that in any case he wants to make the question of Abraham's family central to his argument.

His opening move, in verses 6–9, is to take two key passages from the story of Abraham and to show the direction they are pointing. (We call him 'Abraham' for convenience, as Paul does, even though until Genesis 17.5 his name is simply 'Abram'.) Genesis 15 describes the **covenant** God made with Abraham, promising him a great family, and the land as its inheritance; the critical move was that, when God made the first promise, Abraham believed it. That doesn't mean that his faith *earned* his membership in God's covenant; the promise was already made. It was, rather, the badge that showed he was now in covenant with God. Genesis 15 goes on to promise that this great family would live in a foreign land for a while, and would be brought back to their inheritance by a further great act. The **Exodus**, in other words, is in view from the start.

If Genesis 15 speaks of faith as the sign of covenant membership, Genesis 12, the opening of Abraham's story, promises that God will bless all the nations through him. Put the two together, and what do we have? In a short, tight-packed form, we have Paul's whole argument: when people believe the gospel of Jesus, they are already Abraham's true children. Not only is there no need to abandon faith as the badge of membership and try to ensure it some other way; to do so, like climbing off the back of the tight-rope walker, is to court disaster. Faith is not a temporary badge, to be exchanged for something else later on. It is the sign of membership from one side of the river all the way to the other.

GALATIANS 3.10–14

Redeemed from the Law's Curse

[10]Because, you see, those who belong to the 'works-of-the-law' camp are under a curse! Yes, that's what the Bible says: 'Cursed is everyone who doesn't stick fast by everything written in the book of the law, to perform it.' [11]But, because nobody is justified before God in the law, it's clear that 'the righteous shall live by faith'. [12]The law, however, is not of faith: rather, 'the one who does them shall live in them'.

[13]The Messiah redeemed us from the curse of the law, by becoming a curse on our behalf, as the Bible says: 'Cursed is everyone who hangs on a tree.' [14]This was so that the blessing of Abraham could flow through to the nations in King Jesus – and so that we might receive the promise of the spirit, through faith.

I sat in the traffic jam for two hours. The road signs told me I was pointing in the right direction. From what I knew of the road it looked as though I was in the right place. But nothing was moving. The clock ticked slowly on; I worried about the meeting I was supposed to be getting to; but there was nothing I could do.

Then, quite suddenly, with a hooting of horns, we were on our way. The traffic picked up speed and we were soon moving comfortably down the road. About a mile further on we discovered what had been holding us up. There, by the side of the road, was a huge truck that had overturned. Cranes had now hauled it out of the way, and it lay there, a monument to the blockage that had changed the shape of our day.

It's all very well for Paul to say that believing the **gospel** makes you a child of Abraham, no matter whether you're Jewish or **Gentile**. It was common knowledge among non-Jews as well as among Jews that the Jewish people – Abraham's family, that is – were defined, marked out from their neighbours wherever they went in the world, by the distinguishing marks of what they did. They kept the **sabbaths**. They refused to eat certain foods, the best known being pork. And they **circumcised** their male children, and male converts. This was what the law said, the Jewish **law** that God had given to Moses on Mount Sinai. Those were the terms of the **covenant**. To appeal to Abraham, as it were over the head of Moses, was simply to ignore the main part of the Jewish story, the heart of Jewish practice, a key element in Jewish theology.

But Paul doesn't ignore it. He tells the story differently. He speaks of a gigantic roadblock in the plan of God. God's promise to Abraham wasn't simply about the Jews; it was designed for all the nations. The very opening lines of Genesis 12 said so. That was the road down which the plan was supposed to be going. Abraham's family were to bring God's plan of salvation to the rest of the world. That's why there was such a family in the first place.

But what had happened to this family? And what, in consequence, had happened to God's plan and promise?

Here and elsewhere, Paul is quite clear on his answer: the physical family of Abraham, the Jewish people, had overturned like a huge truck in the road, and were now blocking the original intention. God's promise still held good; God still intended to bless the whole world through Abraham's family; but Israel, the promise-bearers, were not only themselves failing, but getting in the way of the wider fulfilment. In this admittedly dense little paragraph, Paul shows how God has dealt with both aspects of this problem through the death of Jesus and the gift of the spirit – which usually, in his thinking, are the ways in which God does what was necessary to bring his plan to fulfilment.

What has caused Israel to overturn in the road is the law itself. Given as the road map for God's people, it contained rules of the road which warned that certain types of behaviour would result in being cursed rather than blessed. ('Blessing' was of course the original purpose of the covenant; 'curse' is its direct opposite.) This wasn't because God was being stingy or mean; it was more like saying 'if you take this bend at above 50 miles per hour you will crash the truck'. And the curse in question wasn't a kind of other-worldly curse, a condemnation that would simply destroy fellowship with God in the present and blissful life with him hereafter. In Deuteronomy, the main book from which Paul here quotes, the 'curse' is something that will happen in history: Israel will go into **exile**, away from the promised land. The curse of exile – the people of God devastated and deported by the pagan nations – looks uncomfortably like the exact opposite of what God had in mind, that he would bless those nations through Israel. The promises aren't getting through. The road is well and truly blocked.

Meanwhile, Israel's scriptures themselves proclaim that there is a different way through to the promise. Habakkuk, writing at a time when Israel was being devastated, speaks of **faith** as the only way to life – while Leviticus continues to stress that doing the law is essential for life within the law. But what will happen when the law itself has overturned the people who were bearing the promise?

Ah, says Paul, watch what God has done. The curse of which Deuteronomy spoke has been borne by Israel's representative, the **Messiah**. He has come to the point of the roadblock, the point where the pagan nations were oppressing God's people. What was the symbol of that oppression in the first century? Easy: the cross on which the Romans executed tens of thousands of those who opposed them. Jesus, as Israel's Messiah, took the weight of Israel's curse on himself, not just in some abstract theological sense but quite literally and historically, when he died on the cross.

The double result is exactly what was needed. First, the roadblock has been taken out of the way. The traffic can flow as God always intended it: from the promise to Abraham, through his family, his 'seed' (in the person of Israel's representative, the Messiah), and out to all the nations. 'The blessing of Abraham comes on the nations in the Messiah, Jesus': that's Paul's short-hand way of putting it.

Second, ethnic Israel is not left in the ditch, nor simply shunted to one side. What Israel needed, according to prophets like Jeremiah, Ezekiel, Joel and others (each of whom Paul refers to regularly in his writings), was for the covenant to be renewed at last: for God to pour out his **spirit** on Israel and enable it to believe, and so, set upright again, to join the stream of traffic flowing down the road to God's promised inheritance. Fine, says Paul, and that is what has now happened: 'so that we' (that is, Jews who believe the gospel) 'might receive the promise of the spirit through faith.' The cross of Jesus and the gift of the spirit mean that God has dealt with the problem that stood in the way of the blessing reaching out into the world, and embracing Israel as well as it did so.

What roadblocks are there in the way of God's blessing

reaching the world today? How can the fact of the cross and the gift of the spirit be applied to them?

GALATIANS 3.15–22

Christ the Seed, Christ the Mediator

[15]My brothers and sisters, let me use a human illustration. When someone makes a covenanted will, nobody sets it aside or adds to it. [16]Well, the promises were made 'to Abraham and his family'. It doesn't say 'his families', as though referring to several, but indicates one: 'and to your family' – which means the Messiah.

[17]This is what I mean. God made this covenanted will; the law, which came 430 years later, can't undermine it and make the promise null and void. [18]If the inheritance came through the law, it would no longer be by promise; but God gave it to Abraham by promise.

[19]Why then the law? It was added because of transgressions, until the family should come to whom it had been promised. It was laid down by angels, at the hand of a mediator. [20]He, however, is not the mediator of the 'one' – but God is one!

[21]Is the law then against God's promises? Of course not! No, if a law had been given that could have given life, then covenant membership really would have been by the law. [22]But the Bible shut up everything together under the power of sin, so that the promise – which comes by the faithfulness of Jesus the Messiah – should be given to those who believe.

'It's what he would have wanted.' How often has that phrase been used to settle an argument, when someone has died and the family are trying to organize the funeral, or the disposal of property, or the appropriate way to bring up orphaned children. Family disputes about 'what so-and-so would have wanted' can sometimes be as difficult as disputes about the inheritance itself. All clergy know the frustration of trying to organize a service which includes the music, readings and other bits and pieces which the deceased 'would have liked'. How much more satisfactory, as the lawyers keep reminding people, to have it all set out in black and white so there's no question.

Paul's argument here is that God has set out in black and white what he wants and intends, and no subsequent disputes can alter it. The point he's making is that the Galatian 'agitators' are like people at a funeral trying to smuggle in their own agendas – particularly their desire for a strong ethnic Israel without any fraternizing with uncircumcised **Gentiles** – under the guise of 'what he would have wanted'. The strength of their case seems to be that the **law** – which God, after all, gave to Israel through Moses – seems to be on their side. Paul's counter-argument is that if the original **covenant** is clear there can be no question of changing it, and the law must have a different purpose altogether.

What then was God's original intention? That Abraham should have a single worldwide family, consisting of a group defined in terms not of parentage or ethnicity but of **faith**. That's what Paul declared, on the basis of Genesis 12 and 15, in verses 6–9. Now he explores what that means in practice.

The problem with this passage, which emerges in most translations, is the word 'seed', which I have here translated as 'family'. This is in fact the only way to make full sense of Paul's argument. God made promises 'to Abraham and his seed'; the 'seed' is singular, meaning the **Messiah** – who, for Paul, represents God's people, so that the 'singular seed' means *the single family, incorporated into the Messiah, that God always intended*. This was God's covenanted will, and nothing in **heaven** or on earth can shake it. Certainly the law, a comparative latecomer on the scene, cannot do so. The promise comes first and must stand.

I was once teaching Galatians to a class in Montreal, and one of my brightest students – a young clergyman from Kenya – burst out at this point: 'But why then did God give the law?'

As I answered at the time, if that's the question you are left with, you have obviously been following Paul accurately, because that's the question he comes to as well in verse 19. And the answer he gives is that the law was *a necessary part of the intervening story* – intervening, that is, between the giving of the promise and its fulfilment. Though many of Paul's readers have assumed that he regarded the law as a bad thing to be swept aside, this is a total misunderstanding. To see the point we need to grasp something vital in Paul's thought which he only hints at in this passage.

Paul is quite clear that the human race as a whole is sinful, under God's judgment. He is also clear that God called Abraham so that eventually, through his family, the remedy might be found for the problem of human beings and indeed the cosmos as a whole. But Abraham's family from that day onwards were also, still, part of the human race. The people who carried the solution were themselves part of the problem. The doctors were themselves infected with the disease.

What then had to happen? Answer: the doctors themselves needed to be put in quarantine until the medicine they were carrying could be applied. The law was a kind of temporary quarantine for this purpose; to go on insisting on it after the solution has been found is absurd. The law was given, Paul says, because of this in-between state of Abraham's physical family, the people of Israel. It was given, in fact, 'because of transgressions'; a 'transgression' is not just a sin, an act of wickedness, but the breaking of a law. It was given for a set period of time, until the single family intended and promised by God should arrive with the Messiah.

The point of the very difficult verses 19 and 20 is then as follows. The law was given through the agency not only of angels (this is, for Paul, a way of saying that the law was indeed God's law, wonderful and holy) but also of the 'mediator', that is, Moses. Moses, though, cannot be the mediator through whom God creates the 'one', the single family he always wanted; but

God is one, and so (as Paul explains in Romans 3.29–30) he desires a single family, not many families. Left to itself, the law, putting Israel in quarantine as it did, would have created at least two families (Israel, and believing Gentiles; this was the situation in Antioch when Peter and the others separated from the Christian Gentiles), and possibly many more, if the principle had been accepted that different groups of Christians were to be classified by ethnic origin. This cannot have been God's intention.

Once again we ourselves face the question to which Paul is leading us. (These questions, in Paul, are never just answering problems; they are always advancing our understanding a further step.) Doesn't it seem that the law is *against* God's promises?

Certainly not. On the contrary: the problem is not with the law, but with the condition of Abraham's physical family. They, like the rest of the human race, were sinners and so doomed to die. If the law's regulations had been able to deal with that problem, well and good: the covenant would have been fulfilled then and there. But, as Paul already said in 2.21, this wasn't the case. The law didn't have that effect. It was simply a quarantine regulation, important and healthy in itself but a steady reminder that all the human race, including the family of Abraham, was sinful. And it was in place, doing that job, right up to the time when God finally fulfilled the promise.

When he did so, it was not through the law but through the faithfulness of the representative Israelite, Jesus the Messiah. In him, the promise has now come true, not for one ethnic group only, but for all who believe, Jew and Gentile alike. Paul is here very close to what he says in Romans 3.21–26. This is what God had in mind all along: a worldwide family whose badge would be their faith. That family is now created in the Messiah; the Galatians have come to belong to it through their faith in Jesus as Messiah and Lord; they need nothing more to make them full members. Indeed, to go back under the law would be to live once more under the quarantine regulations designed for the interim period.

This passage has much to teach us about the security of all who believe the **gospel**. They are all members of the true people of God, irrespective of racial background. This is a lesson the church still needs to learn. It also helps us to understand something of how to read the Old Testament from a Christian point of view. The Old Testament was God-given, and remains part of Christian scripture; let there be no doubt about that, no attempt to make Paul say anything else. But, precisely because of the Christian story of God's dealings with his people from Abraham onwards, the regulations designed to keep Israel as it were in quarantine are now set aside. Not because they were bad, ill-judged, unnecessary or not intended by God; but because they were good, vital, effective and have now completed their task.

GALATIANS 3.23–29

The Coming of Faith

[23]Before this faithfulness arrived, we were kept under guard by the law, in close confinement until the coming faithfulness should be revealed. [24]Thus the law was like a babysitter for us, looking after us until the coming of the Messiah, so that we might be given covenant membership on the basis of faithfulness.

[25]But now that faithfulness has come, we are no longer under the rule of the babysitter. [26]For you are all children of God through the faithfulness which is in the Messiah, Jesus.

[27]You see, every one of you who has been baptized into the Messiah has put on the Messiah. [28]There is no longer Jew or Greek; there is no longer slave or free; there is no 'male and female'; you are all one in the Messiah, Jesus.

[29]And, if you belong to the Messiah, you are Abraham's family. You stand to inherit the promise.

One of the worst evenings of my daughter's young life was when she was asked to be a babysitter for some friends – a job she had often done before, happily and successfully. Unknown to them or us, the two young children were in a very cross mood, and resented their parents going out for the evening. They took out their sulks and anger on my daughter. She had a miserable time, but managed to prevent the children getting up to anything too drastically wicked. She – and, I think, the children – were extremely relieved when the evening was over.

Paul's picture of the **law** in Israel's story now focuses on its task and role as a babysitter until Israel should grow up. The word I have translated as 'babysitter' would normally, in Paul's world, refer to a slave whose task it was to look after the children day by day on the parents' behalf, taking them to school, making sure they were safe, keeping them out of mischief and so on. Many cultures still have such people, who sometimes become honoured members of the family after their child-related duties come to an end. In the Western world, this role is sometimes taken by an au pair.

Paul's basic point is about the story of Israel between the time of Moses and the coming of the **Messiah**. During this time, *Israel was still a child and needed special looking after*. The fact that Israel needed a babysitter during the period of childhood did not mean that the babysitter should continue to do the job once the child had grown up. And what Paul is claiming throughout the letter is that, with the coming of the Messiah, Israel was at last God's grown-up child. Israel had reached the age of responsibility, or trustworthiness. And the word for 'trustworthiness' is the same as '**faith**'. Paul can thus declare that 'faith' – the same word in Greek can mean 'faithfulness', 'trust', 'trustworthiness', 'reliability' – is the sign of maturity, in other words, the sign that the babysitter is no longer needed. The faithfulness of the Messiah himself is the sign that here at last is a mature Israelite, come to bring God's promises to fulfilment. The answering faith of the believer is the sign that this person, no matter what their ethnic background, is a full and complete member of God's family.

So he explains, in verse 26: all of you are children of God, through this faithfulness, in the Messiah, Jesus. 'Children of God' is itself a biblical title for Israel: Israel, said God, is my son, my firstborn (Exodus 4.22). That is to say, this title goes with the great story of the **Exodus**, God's redemption of Israel from slavery in Egypt, which Paul will draw on in the next stage of his argument (4.1–7). Paul is now beginning to take that story, the foundation of all that Israel knew about itself as God's redeemed people, and move it on a stage further. The whole of Israel's history from Moses to the Messiah, he will declare, has been like the time when Israel was enslaved in Egypt. Now the time of deliverance has come. Do you want to go back to being a child, when you could be grown-up? Do you want to go back to being a slave, when you could be free? And the badge of the grown-up child of God, the badge of God's free people, is that he trusts them with responsibility: they are people of faith, of trust. They believe the **gospel**.

But how can belonging to the Messiah's people give them this status of being God's grown-up children? Paul explains in a dense, sometimes bewildering, passage. When he uses the word '**Christ**', not only does he mean 'Messiah', but he also means that the Messiah is the one who sums Israel up in himself. What matters for Paul is that someone is 'in' the Messiah, or 'belongs to' the Messiah. This is not simply a spiritual state resulting from, or consisting in, a certain type of inner experience. For Paul, it is a matter of belonging to a particular community, the new royal family, the Messiah's people; and this family is entered through **baptism**.

Baptism is therefore 'into the Messiah': it is the doorway through which one passes into membership in the single family God promised to Abraham. Paul does not here explain how baptism relates to faith; he assumes they are both present, as indeed he would, since 'Jesus is Lord' was what the candidate for baptism would have to say. Nor does he discuss, as he does in 1 Corinthians 10, the problems that arise from people being baptized who seem not to realize what it involves.

Those who are baptized have thus 'put on the Messiah'. They are the Messiah's family. As a result, old distinctions cease to be relevant in terms of their status in the family, their standing before God or one another. This is not to say that every aspect of their human identity becomes irrelevant; Paul is still aware of himself as a Jewish Christian (see, e.g., Romans 11.1–6), but this is not the basis of his standing as part of the true family of Abraham. He is still aware of some people being slaves and others free, or why would he have written the letter to Philemon? He is still aware of maleness and femaleness, as numerous passages indicate. But the point is that *all these are irrelevant for your status in Christ*. The ground is even, as has often been said, at the foot of the cross. 'You are all one in the Messiah, Jesus.'

Then comes the great conclusion to the whole chapter. Paul's point is precisely that God promised Abraham a single family, and that, in the Messiah, God has at last created just that. 'If you belong to the Messiah, you are Abraham's family.' Why look anywhere else? Why try to become a child of Abraham by any other means? But, if you are part of Abraham's family, you stand to inherit under the terms of God's original covenanted will (3.15–18).

The passage speaks powerfully to every situation in which – as is, sadly, far more common than in Paul's day – the church is divided along ethnic or cultural lines. Most of the great divisions in Christendom – Eastern Orthodox over against the Western churches (i.e. Rome and the churches that broke away from Rome); the protestantism of northern Europe and its colonies against the catholicism of southern Europe and its offshoots; the vestigial Scottish/English division of presbyterian and episcopalian; and many of the newer free churches, often reflecting different cultures and social types – most of these divisions, though understandable historically, fall under God's judgment when considered in the light of this chapter. A passion for Paul's gospel translates directly into a passion for the unity of the church.

Equally, Paul's argument about the immature and mature people of God leads to some probing questions of ourselves as individuals and as churches. Are we truly grown-up? Are we trustworthy? Do we really believe? Or would we secretly prefer to be looked after by a babysitter?

GALATIANS 4.1–7

The Son and the Spirit

¹Let me put it like this. As long as the heir is a child, he is no different from a slave – even if, in fact, he is master of everything! ²He is kept under guardians and stewards until the time set by his father.

³Well, it's like that with us. When we were children, we were kept in 'slavery' under the 'elements of the world'. ⁴But when the time of fulfilment arrived, God sent out his son, born of a woman, born under the law, ⁵so that he might redeem those under the law, so that we might receive adoption as sons.

⁶And, because you are sons, God sent out the spirit of his son into our hearts, calling out 'Abba, father!' ⁷So you are no longer a slave, but a son! And, if you're a son, you are an heir, through God.

If you've ever tried to write a story, you have probably discovered that your characters get themselves into muddles from which it's quite hard to get them out. Several nineteenth-century novelists faced this problem, often with heroes and heroines getting into financial and family problems without any obvious solution. A favourite way out of the puzzle was to resolve matters by having someone previously unmentioned die and leave one of the characters a large inheritance. Near the end of the novel, a message arrives to say that a long-forgotten uncle or cousin, perhaps on the other side of the world, has died and left them a fortune. Suddenly everything is resolved. We can breathe again. New hope is born, problems are forgotten, and everyone celebrates.

We may smile at the ease with which a novelist can get a character out of trouble, and produce a happy ending to the story, by such a simple device that has nothing to do with the rest of the plot. Today's serious fiction normally frowns on such a trick – perhaps because we live in a world with considerably fewer rich but forgotten uncles. But part of the appeal of that twist in the plot – as well as the dream that many cherish, that something unexpected will turn up and settle all their problems at a stroke – is the fact that it bears a striking similarity to the story Paul tells in this passage, a story so central to Christianity that, even where Paul's writings are not studied, the story itself is well known.

The story is precisely of people who stand to inherit a fortune (of sorts) but who are quite unaware of the fact. There are two categories of people who are to inherit it jointly; they come from different backgrounds, but they will be together at the end. Jewish Christians, in other words, and **Gentile** Christians, each come from a very different starting point, but for Paul that ceases to matter when they become Christians. Like one person who arrives at church on Sunday morning by walking across the street, and another who arrives by helicopter from the next county, their journeys are very different but their goal is the same.

Paul begins where he left off at the end of the previous argument: with the son who is also the heir. He considers, within this picture, the condition of such a person before reaching the age of maturity: the father appoints trustees and guardians to look after him, much like the babysitter in the previous paragraph (3.24–25). The task Paul sets himself now is to develop this thought in relation to two others: first, the act of God in the new **Exodus**, the great and final act of redemption, accomplished in **Christ** and by the **spirit**; second, the parallel journey of Jews and Gentiles, from parallel conditions of slavery, on their way to **faith** and freedom. We must look at these two in turn before putting the paragraph back together again.

These verses are full of the language of Exodus. God called Moses to lead Israel out of slavery in Egypt into freedom, to inherit the promised land. After a long period of waiting, already predicted in Genesis 15, the time of fulfilment came: God sent Moses to redeem his people, that is, to purchase their freedom from slavery. This was also to demonstrate that, as Moses said to Pharaoh, 'Israel is my son, my firstborn.' Freedom was secured through Passover, with the sacrifice of the lambs and the slaying of Egypt's firstborn. Then, when the people had left Egypt, they came to Sinai, 40 days after Passover; and they were given the **law** as their guide through the wilderness to their inheritance. That is the story that every Jew knows, and that forms the foundation for a great many Jewish writings ancient and modern.

Imagine this story as a picture painted on a sheet of glass, so that you can still see through the glass while looking at the picture that's on it. Hold this painted glass to your eye, look at the story Paul is telling in this paragraph, and see what happens. Israel is in slavery – but now the slavemasters are not the Egyptians, but 'the elements of the world', an unusual phrase which probably refers to the guardian angels or deities which, in Jewish thought, looked after the different nations. In one of his most daring moves, Paul suggests that the Jewish law itself had become just another guardian angel, looking after Israel and keeping it separate from the other nations – in other words, preventing for the moment any fulfilment of God's long-term intention of freedom and integration, of the creation of the single worldwide family.

But then comes the new Passover. God sent out, not Moses, but his own son, Jesus the **Messiah**, so that through his death freedom could be bought and the slaves could become true children. Not only so: 40 days after Passover, on the feast of Pentecost, God gave, not the law, but his own spirit, the spirit of his son, to turn his people into his true children in their innermost beings as well as in legal status. The evidence of this is that, when the spirit has been at work, the prayer which arises unbidden from their hearts is the prayer of Jesus, calling God by the familiar Aramaic name, *Abba*, Daddy. (*Abba* was used by adult Jewish children as well as young ones; the point is not the age of the child, but the intimacy and familiarity of the word.)

The people of Israel in Egypt suddenly discovered that their God had an inheritance for them, and was going to set them free from slavery and lead them to this inheritance. Now, Paul says, this is what has happened, only in a deeper and final way, to Jews and Gentiles alike. By telling the story this way he has been able to hint, also, that the story of God's redeeming of the child is true as much for Gentiles as for Jews – because the Gentiles have also, of course, been subject to the guardian angels, the deities appointed to look after them.

Thus, though in verse 3 Paul is talking about Jews ('we'), what he says about these Jews who have become Christians is designed to make their story as alike as possible to that of Gentile Christians. His aim throughout is to make the Galatians, themselves of course Gentile Christians, realize that their pilgrimage from paganism to Christian faith is matched, stride for stride, by the Jewish pilgrimage from the 'young child' status, under the law, into Christian faith. Of course there are differences. The Jew was already following the same God who has now been revealed in Jesus and by the spirit, whereas the pagan was following idols (see the next paragraph). But the routes are parallel, and the destination is identical.

In the Exodus, the God of Abraham revealed himself in a new way as the **covenant**-keeping God, the God who heard the cry of his people and came down to rescue them. The book of Exodus itself sees this as the revealing of God's personal name, YHWH (Exodus 3.14; 6.2–8). Now, in a move as bold as it is original, Paul declares that, through his action in Jesus and the spirit, the one God of Abraham has now made himself known, not just by name and action, but in personal presence as a human among humans, a Jew among Jews. God's son Jesus, and the spirit of God's son, are both sent out from God, not as beings remote or detached from himself, but as his own self-revelation, his own personal presence. Though theologians did not use the word 'trinity', and the technical terms associated with it, until some time later than Paul, the roots of the three-in-one Christian understanding of God are already present in this, one of the earliest, if not *the* earliest, document we possess from the young church.

In the last verse of this paragraph Paul suddenly shifts from the second person plural to the second person singular. '*You*,' he says, pointing a finger at the reader: you, not the person sitting next to you; you are no longer a slave, but a true child and heir. Until each reader has heard that word addressed to him- or herself, the message has not got through. Paul the writer remained a preacher, and Paul the preacher knew how to ram the point home.

GALATIANS 4.8–11

The True God and the False Gods

[8]However, at that stage you didn't know God, and so you were enslaved to beings that, in their proper nature, are not gods. [9]But now that you've come to know God – or, better, to be known *by* God – how can you turn back again to that weak and poverty-stricken line-up that you want to serve all over again? [10]You are observing days, and months, and seasons, and years! [11]I am afraid for you; perhaps my hard work with you is all going to be wasted.

The whale is one of the greatest sights in the animal kingdom. To go out on a small boat, to wait perhaps for hours, and then to see one of these magnificent creatures come to the surface, or even leap from the water – few can resist the experience. And one of the wonderful things about it is that these animals are free. They are doing what they want to do, living their own lives.

But, of course, some whales live in captivity. Some are kept in great aquariums, where they are (usually) well looked after, regularly fed, and taught to do remarkable things. They are intelligent animals, and enjoy working and playing with humans, and showing off in front of an audience.

Not everyone, though, approves of keeping them in captivity. Some years ago, on the Pacific coast of North America, animal rights activists managed to set a whale free from an aquarium beside the ocean. What happened next was remarkable. The whale swam some distance, spent a short time at sea, and then returned voluntarily to the aquarium. It had obviously decided that it was better off being looked after in captivity than fending for itself in the dangerous and difficult world outside.

That was the choice that faced the children of Israel under Moses. They had come out of slavery in Egypt, under the leadership of Moses, and now they faced a long journey into an unknown future. Often they didn't know where the next meal was coming from; and when they did have regular food they quickly got tired of it. They were afraid, first of the pursuing Egyptians, then of the Canaanites who were defending the promised land. Again and again the cry went up: why did we leave Egypt? We were better off as slaves than following this crazy dream (Exodus 14.11–12; 16.3; 17.3; Numbers 14.1–4)! Sometimes they actually plotted to choose a different leader and go back to Egypt, like the whale returning to captivity.

This picture of the wilderness wanderings lies behind Paul's impassioned appeal in this passage. The Galatian Christians have come out of the 'Egypt' of idolatry, of worshipping false gods. They have been set free, redeemed by the personal action

48

of the one true God in his son and his **spirit** (4.4–7). Now, it seems, they have had a look at the wide and worrying world of freedom, and they don't like what they see. They are determined to return once more to the world where life seems safer, more regulated, where you know where you are: in other words, to the life of slavery. They are, Paul declares, choosing to go back where they were before, back to the old pagan gods they had worshipped until the time when they were set free by the living God.

On the face of it, this is an astonishing claim. The Galatians aren't starting to worship their old pagan deities; they are wanting to become Jews. But Paul is adamant. Now that the **Messiah** has come, and with him the new world where God's grace reaches out to all alike, if they try to embrace Judaism they are declaring their preference for a system in which ethnic and territorial membership matters rather than membership in the Messiah's new family. They are opting for the rule of the Jewish **law**, which had kept Israel in a state of virtual slavery from Moses to the Messiah (3.23–25; 4.3). They are as good as saying that they prefer to be ruled by the old line-up of deities which kept the different nations under their sway, rather than by the true God who has now revealed, in action, who he really is.

Paul is quite clear that the Jewish law was given *by* God, with a purpose within his overall plan. But now that the plan has been fulfilled, anyone who goes back to the earlier stage is treating the law as though it were something independent that could stand for all time; treating it, in other words, as a god. And the Galatians ought to know that the whole point of becoming a Christian was to escape from the rule of the enslaving 'gods', and to find freedom in knowing the true God.

Or rather, in being known by this true God. Paul corrects himself in verse 9, because, as he says in 1 Corinthians 8.2–3, what really matters is not your knowledge of God, but God's knowledge of you. Our knowledge of God is small, feeble, and partial, and seems to go up and down with our moods and feelings. If that was the thing that made us Christians, we would be building on very shaky foundations. What matters is that God has 'known' us; not just in the sense that he knows *about* us, though that of course is true as well, but that he has, from his own side of the relationship, established a bond, a **covenant**, in which he knows us through and through, and names us as his own family.

The choice is then clear. You either continue in freedom, being known by the God who has revealed himself as father, son and spirit (4.4–7). Or you turn back, become an idolater again, and so become enslaved as you were before. The primary snare for the Christian is not breaking moral laws, important though that is, but the idolatry – the worshipping of false gods – that leads to such behaviour. That is the focus of Paul's plea here. Make sure you're worshipping the true God, and everything else will follow.

The symptom of their rebellion that he highlights is one he doesn't mention elsewhere, but obviously it was becoming important in the muddled life of the young Galatian Christians. 'You observe', he says, 'days, months, seasons and years!' Now from very early on the Christian church kept various festivals: Paul himself speaks of the first day of the week as special (1 Corinthians 16.2), and certainly the early Christians met on what they called 'the Lord's day' (Revelation 1.10), the day that had been made special for ever by Jesus' **resurrection**. Likewise, Easter quickly became an important annual festival; and many in the church, including Paul himself (Acts 20.6, 16; 1 Corinthians 16.8), continued to date what they were doing by reference to Jewish festivals such as Passover and Pentecost. So it can't be that all observances of days and times was to be banned. In any case, Paul himself says in Romans 14.5–6 that observing days or not observing them is something for individual Christians to decide as a matter of their own personal discipleship.

What seems to matter here is that the Galatians are insisting on keeping the Jewish festivals; and the point of those Jewish festivals was that they all looked forward to the great act of redemption which God would one day accomplish. So how can they keep them when God's future has already arrived in Jesus **Christ**? They are saying, by these observances, that they aren't sure if God really has done what he said he would – whereas the whole point of the **gospel** is that he has! This is what makes Paul say, with exasperation, that he is beginning to wonder if he's wasted all his effort over them.

But the heart of the passage, and perhaps its central thrust for Christians today, is the call to find true freedom in knowing and being known by the true God. The life of devotion and worship, gazing in adoration at the true God whose character and actions we can never study enough, sets us free from the rule of other gods – but the other gods will continually whisper to us that we might actually prefer being enslaved to them again. It's easier to rule your life by the old line-up of options: racial or tribal identity, geographical or territorial loyalty, the demands of money, sex and power. It's much harder to follow the God revealed in Jesus and the spirit, and to learn true freedom, true humanness, in the fellowship of other followers. But, as Paul will go on to say, there really is no alternative. God has acted; we have tasted the effect of that action. If we go back now, we are denying not only ourselves and our Christian experience, but God himself.

GALATIANS 4.12–20

Paul's Appeal to His Children

[12]Become like me! – because I became like you, my dear family. This is my plea to you. You didn't wrong me: [13]no, you know that it was through bodily weakness that I announced the gospel to you in the first place. [14]You didn't despise or ridicule me, even though my condition was quite a test for you, but

you welcomed me as if I were God's angel, as if I were the Messiah, Jesus! [15]What's happened to the blessing you had then? Yes, I can testify that you would have torn out your eyes, if you'd been able to, and given them to me. [16]So have I become your enemy by telling you the truth?

[17]The other lot are eager for you, but it's not in a good cause. They want to shut you out, so that you will then be eager for them. [18]Well, it's always good to be eager in a good cause, and not only when I'm there with you. [19]My children – I seem to be in labour with you all over again, until the Messiah is fully formed in you! [20]I wish I were there with you right now, and could change my tone of voice. I really am at a loss about you.

The French teacher was a strict disciplinarian. We weren't allowed to speak a word of English during the classes, and neither did he. Everything, even trivial comments or requests, had to be made in French. He was determined that we would not only learn to read, write and speak in French, but come to think in it as well.

So we were all the more startled when one day he walked into the class, stood in front of us, and quietly spoke in English. We'd never heard him do that before. He was very angry. We had all done very badly in our examination the previous week. The only way he could make the point with sufficient shock value was to break his normal pattern and to talk in English, as though he were saying to us, 'You've done so badly in French that maybe I can't even speak to you in it any more.' It made a deep impression. Then, after a few minutes, he resumed the normal lesson.

This is the point in Galatians where Paul, as it were, stops talking theology, breaks off his train of thought, and speaks in quite a different way to his surprised hearers. Up until this point, at least since 2.15, he has been mounting a step-by-step argument, requiring his hearers (not to mention his readers 2,000 years later!) to follow it closely and think hard. Now, quite suddenly, like a teacher stopping the lesson, coming to the front of the class, taking off his spectacles and speaking to the pupils directly, he tells them what he's thinking, how it feels, what sort of thoughts are rushing through his head at a more personal level. This is a heart-to-heart moment. Almost every line is an appeal to friendship, to family loyalty, to a mutual bond established by their common experience of what God has done for them together.

It all goes back to the time when Paul first arrived in Galatia. He was in bad shape. We don't know what the problem was: some think he was sick, others that he had been badly beaten in a recent persecution. (If he was sick, we don't know what sort of sickness it was, though there has been a lot of speculation on the matter.) In any case, his physical condition when he arrived was so bad that it was quite off-putting to the Galatians. But this didn't stop them from welcoming him; in fact, as he announced the **good news** of Jesus, God worked so powerfully through him that they knew they were in the presence of someone extraordinary, and treated him accordingly. 'As though I were an angel,' he says; 'as though I were the **Messiah** himself, Jesus in person.'

The underlying point here seems to be that Paul is reminding them that his 'flesh', his physical condition, was no problem for them at that stage. Now, therefore, they ought not to suppose that their own 'flesh', their present condition, i.e. uncircumcision, will be any problem to him or to anyone else. Whether it be personality cults, fine clothes, physical **circumcision**, wealth, noble birth, social status – whatever it is, it's all irrelevant when it comes to preaching the **gospel**, hearing the gospel, or living by the gospel. Paul wants them to see that just as he, a Jew, has been cheerfully prepared to suffer for the gospel, so they should be prepared to share his status, that of being defined simply and solely by their **faith** in Jesus **Christ**.

So, he asks, what has gone wrong? What happened to that blessing, that wonderful state of opening their hearts and lives to the word and power of the gospel, and finding it transform them from within? At the time they would have done anything for him (to speak of 'plucking out your eyes for someone' was a regular way of saying 'I would do anything for you'). Now, since all he's done is tell them the truth, surely they aren't going to turn away from him? This is a direct appeal to the loyalty of friendship. Theological argument is important; but unless it takes place within a context where people are bonded together in mutual trust and shared Christian experience, it will only reach the head, not the heart, and probably not the will.

The real reason for the break – or the potential break – in their relationship has been the other people who have come in. Paul here only speaks of them as 'they', but it's clear what these people want to do. They want to shut the Galatians out. Remember chapter 2: they want to set up a two-level fellowship, an outer circle for **Gentile** Christians and an inner circle for Jewish Christians. That way they can present themselves to their Jewish friends or family as proper, **law**-abiding Jews; and they will then compel the Galatians to come, cap in hand, to seek circumcision as the price of admission to the inner circle.

But Paul knows that there can be no outer circle and inner circle within the grace of God. 'They', he says, 'are eager for you'; the word he uses for 'eager' is actually 'zealous', filled with the zeal that he himself had once had, zeal for God and the law, zeal to make converts to Judaism. But Paul is now using the word in a wider sense as well. Zeal in this wider sense is a good thing: it is fine to burn with eagerness for God's work, but it must be on the right lines (compare Romans 10.2, where he describes his fellow Jews as having a zeal for God, but not according to knowledge). Paul wants them to be on fire with love for God, for the gospel, for the fellowship of all other believers. The zeal that 'they', the opponents or agitators, are exhibiting is of another kind: they are aflame with eagerness to consolidate their view of God's people as a family based principally on ethnic, physically marked membership.

Faced with this, Paul is almost in despair. What can he do? What can he say to make them change their minds? He feels like a mother who, after giving birth, finds herself going through labour pains all over again, watching her children struggle to become the mature adults they were supposed to be. Here he describes his aim for them very strikingly: 'until the Messiah is formed in you'. His goal is that the messianic life – the self-giving love which embraces all alike – should appear in their own community. If only he could be there in person and explain it all to them kindly, sympathetically, with the language of face and body that would tell them how much he loved them; that would win from them an answering love and trust! Letters are a poor substitute for personal presence, though they have spin-off value: if Paul hadn't written Galatians, we wouldn't have all this wealth of insight and teaching.

This little section, then, stands here in Galatians as witness to the marriage of head and heart in the teaching and pastoral work that belong to the gospel. We may convince people's minds, but unless we can look them in the eye (or make them feel, through other types of communication, that that is what's happening), we may have little effect. Paul, one of the greatest ever theologians, knew that what really mattered was the formation of the Messiah's own life in this community, the life in which there was neither Jew nor Greek. He was determined to make the point by every available means. He now returns to theological argument, having reminded them that he is not just a brain with a mouth attached, but a warm-hearted human being with a primary claim on their love and loyalty.

GALATIANS 4.21–31

Abraham's Two Sons

[21]So, you want to live under the law, do you? All right, tell me this: are you prepared to hear what the law says? [22]For the Bible

says that Abraham had two sons, one by the slave-girl and one by the free woman. [23]Now the child of the slave-girl was born according to the flesh, while the child of the free woman was born according to promise.

[24]Treat this as picture-language. These two women stand for two covenants: one comes from Mount Sinai, and is born into slavery; that is Hagar. [25](Sinai, you see, is a mountain in Arabia, and it corresponds, in the picture, to the present Jerusalem, since she is in slavery with her children.) [26]But the Jerusalem which is above is free – and she is our mother. [27]For the Bible says,

Celebrate, childless one, who never gave birth!
Go wild and shout, girl that never had pains!
The barren woman has many more children
Than the one who has a husband!

[28]Now you, my family, are children of promise, in the line of Isaac. [29]But things now are like they were then: the one who was born according to the flesh persecuted the one born according to the spirit. [30]But what does the Bible say? 'Throw out the slave-girl and her son! For the son of the slave-girl will not inherit with the son of the free.' [31]So, my family, we are not children of the slave-girl, but of the free.

Not long ago, there was an international rugby match played in pouring rain. The pitch became muddier and muddier, and the players got dirtier and dirtier. The spectators couldn't tell which side was which. Then the referee discovered that even he could no longer recognize who was on which side. Finally the players themselves couldn't tell the difference between their own side and the opposition.

So the referee offered them the chance to go and change into clean kit. One side refused: they were proud of their national jerseys, and didn't want to look like cowards, changing out of wet clothes into dry ones. The other side were delighted, and went off to change into warm, dry kit. When they came out again, not only could everyone tell the difference between the two sides; the side in the clean kit felt so much better that they went on to win the match.

By this point in Galatians Paul realizes that there are so many interlocking issues on the table that it's time to sort out what's what. The different elements of the argument have become quite muddy in the debate between himself and his opponents, with the Galatians trying to make sense of it all in between. So he decides on a plan that will make it clear to all concerned just who is on which side.

The opponents have claimed that they have the Jewish **law** on their side. Paul, they have said, has carefully avoided telling the Galatians the full story. If they want to become proper children of Abraham, part of God's true people, then they must follow the law, including getting **circumcised** (the most obvious starting point for **Gentiles**). But Paul has other ideas. He's not going to let them get away with the suggestion that he doesn't know, or follow, the law; the law itself, the first five books of the Bible, tells a story which weighs heavily on his side of the argument. Back he goes to one of the least happy episodes in the Book of Genesis: the story of Abraham's wife and Abraham's concubine, and the sons that each of them bore. And he uses this as a picture of what's going on in his own day.

The story is set out in Genesis 16 and 21. Before the birth of Isaac (though after the promises made in Genesis 15, which form the underlying theme of Galatians 3), Abraham's wife Sarah suggested to him that, according to the customs of the time, he should take her slave-girl as his concubine, and have children by her which would count as Sarah's own. Abraham agreed.

The plan misfired badly. Hagar, the slave-girl in question, became pregnant, and then proceeded to celebrate her superiority to the still barren Sarah. (In that culture, of course, to be childless was shameful for a woman.) Sarah then ill-treated her; Hagar ran away, but relented and came back, and gave birth to a son, Ishmael. Later Sarah, too, became pregnant, after a specific promise from God concerning her (Genesis 17.15–21; 18.9–14); she gave birth to Isaac. Some time later, Sarah became jealous of Ishmael, because of her son Isaac, and dismissed him and his mother. Ishmael became the father of the peoples of Arabia: Isaac was the father of Jacob and Esau, and thence of Israel as a whole.

How can we – or Paul, for that matter – make something of this? How can we sort it all out and decide what in this complex biblical story means what?

It is possible that Paul's opponents had been using this story to reinforce their point that, though the Galatians might in a sense have come into God's people through believing the **gospel**, it looked as if there were now two families, both claiming to be Abraham's children. If that was so, the opponents may have said, they, the Jewish Christians, must be the true, free children, the descendants of Isaac; Gentile Christians, still uncircumcised, must be, in this sense, the children of Ishmael, the outsiders, the foreigners, the people of Arabia as opposed to the citizens of Israel.

Paul stands this on its head, using arguments from Genesis and elsewhere to support his point. All right, he says, supposing Abraham really does have two families: how can you tell which side is which? Which side is really the slave-family, and which is the free?

The key is that the true family – the Isaac-family, in other words – is the one created by God's promise. Abraham and Sarah decided to try having children through Hagar, without any promise of God; Ishmael was therefore born 'according to the flesh'. Isaac, though, was born according to God's promise.

From here on, all the other parts of the picture – the other players on the two teams, if you like – become recognizable. Paul has already shown that the law of Moses, given on Sinai, functioned between the time of Moses and the coming of the **Messiah** to keep the Israelites enslaved (3.23—4.3). The law, therefore, left to itself, produces not Isaac-children, but Ishmael-children.

Paul explains this with a verse which puzzled early scribes, who copied it out in several different ways. What he probably wrote (as in the translation above) is 'For Sinai is a mountain in Arabia'; in other words, the law of Moses, given on Mount Sinai, now corresponds to the outsiders in the original picture. Some scribes, though, wrote it down so that it read 'Hagar is Mount Sinai in Arabia'; but this, ultimately, makes the same point. Hagar, in the story, corresponds to Mount Sinai, the place which symbolizes the law that the Galatian opponents are appealing to.

So far, then, the teams line up as follows:

Isaac	*Ishmael*
➤ promise	➤ flesh
➤ free	➤ slave
	➤ Sinai

Paul will now bring into the story a whole new dimension. His opponents claim authority from Jerusalem; well, maybe so, but they are talking about 'the present Jerusalem', as opposed to the heavenly Jerusalem, 'the Jerusalem above', which is the real home of all believers. To demonstrate this he quotes a text from Isaiah 54, addressed to Jerusalem herself, promising that she, bereft as she had been, would now bear children in profusion. Thus:

➤ Jerusalem above	➤ 'present Jerusalem'
➤ bereft, but now fruitful	➤ in slavery with her children

Then he makes two final moves. First, all those who believe in Jesus, trusting God's promise rather than their 'fleshly' identity, belong on the Isaac-side, while those who claim to represent present Jerusalem belong with Ishmael:

➤ Galatian Christians

➤ trusting in God by the spirit

➤ Jerusalem-based 'agitators'

➤ trusting in 'fleshly' identity

Finally, Ishmael-people will persecute Isaac-people; but they will eventually be cast out. It is the Isaac-family, not the Ishmael-family, who will inherit the promises (this, of course, echoes the end of chapter 3):

➤ Galatian Christians

➤ persecuted

➤ will inherit

➤ Jerusalem-based agitators

➤ persecutors

➤ will be cast out

Paul is not concerned to speculate about the fate of the agitators. The point he wants to emphasize is that 'we' – Paul himself, and those who believe the gospel he has preached – cannot be labelled as outsiders, second-class citizens, or Abraham's illegitimate family. Those who believe the gospel are, like Isaac, promise-people, the free family of God.

GALATIANS 5.1–6

Freedom in Christ

[1]The Messiah set us free so that we could enjoy freedom! So stand firm, and don't get yourselves tied down by the chains of slavery.

[2]Look here: I, Paul, am telling you that if you get circumcised, the Messiah will be of no use to you. [3]I testify once more, against every person who gets circumcised, that they are thereby under obligation to perform the entire law. [4]You are split off from the Messiah, you people who want to be justified

by the law! You have dropped out of grace. ⁵For we are waiting eagerly, by the spirit and by faith, for the hope of righteousness. ⁶For in the Messiah, Jesus, neither circumcision nor uncircumcision has any power. What matters is faith, working through love.

The lake freezes over for four months in the winter, to a depth of at least ten feet. People drive not only snowmobiles across it, but even cars and vans. It's exciting – and also quite convenient – to be able to drive across the water to the village on the opposite shore.

But there comes a time, in late March or early April, when spring comes even to the lakes north of Montreal. Suddenly the ice is not so firm. Wise drivers don't attempt the crossing any more. The villagers leave an old car on the middle of the ice; when it begins to sink, they know the time has come to stop driving across the ice. Soon the lake will be unfrozen; boats will be operating again; and anyone who wants to take the car to the other side will have to put it on the ferry.

Paul's point is this: spring has come to the people of God. For over a thousand years their fellowship with God has been established through the **law**. This was always essentially a winter regime, a time of waiting. There are, so to speak, modes of travel which are appropriate during that winter season. But if you become so keen on them that you don't want to abandon them in spring, you're going to be stuck at the water's edge – or maybe will even risk trying to get across when the ice will no longer hold your weight.

Paul's opponents, to use this illustration, were eager to insist that everyone should cross the lake by car. They had developed all kinds of rules of the road for getting across. The chief thing, for those starting the journey into the Jewish **covenant** community, was for the males to get **circumcised**. This was like starting the engine of the car; it was the sign that they had committed themselves to making the crossing by this route.

But Paul's whole point is that this route is no longer available. Spring has come, the ice has melted, and there is a new way over the lake. And this time spring is for good. God's new age has broken in upon the world, and winter will never come again. The **Messiah** has established the fleet of boats that will take across anyone prepared to leave their old vehicles on the shore.

So if the Galatians – **Gentile** Christians as they are – are persuaded to get themselves circumcised, they are like people being persuaded to start up their cars as though getting ready to drive across the ice when it is already melting through. There is no way across by that means. If you get circumcised, you are committing yourself to keeping the whole law, the entire Jewish **Torah**. It isn't just a minor ritual requirement, which can then go comfortably alongside commitment to the Messiah. That is what the 'agitators' have implied, but Paul with his Pharisaic training can see that this is just the beginning. The only point of getting circumcised is if you are then intending to submit, in every other way as well, to the full discipline of the Jewish synagogue. The only point in starting the car is if you are going to drive it all the way.

For Paul, then, the choice is absolute. You cannot have it both ways. If you want to come with the Messiah – which is now, in fact, the only way across the river – you cannot cling to the law. If you do cling to it, you are declaring that you don't want to belong to the Messiah's people.

The alternative is stated in two great sentences, which sum up what Christianity is all about. First, in verse 5: we are waiting eagerly, by the **spirit**, for the hope of righteousness. Second, in verse 6: neither circumcision nor uncircumcision has any power for those in the Messiah, because what matters is **faith** working through love. These are typically Pauline tight-packed statements. Each needs some elaboration.

The first throws the emphasis towards the future. Paul speaks of the time when God will declare publicly and completely that all those in Christ really are his people. This is 'the hope of righteousness', the longing for the time when God's vindication and **justification** of all his faithful people will be made manifest, the time of the new creation (6.15). And, he says, we await this great event, the conferring of this public status, 'by the spirit' – in other words, not by the 'flesh', the marks of circumcision made in the human body. In other words, if you want evidence here and now that our future hope is not in vain, you should find such evidence not in the status you attain through having a minor physical operation but in the new life you have in the spirit. In terms of the illustration, the spirit is the ticket that guarantees us a place on the boat which, unlike the car, will now be able to cross the river.

This already goes some way to explaining verse 6. What matters is not being circumcised, nor yet being uncircumcised. Paul will repeat this in 6.15; this is what, on the negative side, he most wants the Galatians to grasp. The physical marks of membership in Abraham's family, or the absence of such marks, are not the point. What matters (as he has said all along) is faith.

But it is not a bare faith, simply giving credence to a set of beliefs. It is a faith that works – but not with 'the works of the law'. You cannot get across the lake partly in a boat and partly in a car. It is faith that works through love. Love is open to all, no matter of what ethnic origin; but, even more, love is precisely the motivating force through which God himself welcomes all believers into his family. That same motivating force is what ought to make all family members welcome one another as well.

GALATIANS 5.7–12

Warnings Against Compromise

[7]You were running well. Who got in your way and stopped you being persuaded by the truth? [8]This persuasion didn't come

from the one who called you! [9]A little leaven leavens the whole lump. [10]I am persuaded in the Lord that you won't differ from me on this. But the one who is troubling you will bear the blame, whoever he may be. [11]As for me, my dear family, if I am still announcing circumcision, why am I still being persecuted? If I were, the scandal of the cross would have been neutralized. [12]If only those who are making trouble for you would cut the whole lot off!

One of the few times I watch television is when I'm travelling, and find myself in a strange place, with my body-clock telling me I should be awake when it's the middle of the night. Sitting in a hotel room, and wishing I could go to sleep, I sometimes flip through the television channels, hoping for something interesting to watch. After a while it becomes confusing: the brain finds itself jumping to and fro from a basketball game to a courtroom, to a domestic scene, to a car chase, to a lecture, to an advertisement, and back to another basketball game. The effect, of course, is that the mind becomes so confused that it's harder to go to sleep.

Perhaps that's the effect Paul intends to create with this sharp, jerky little paragraph. We move bewilderingly from athletics, to the courtroom, to the kitchen, to meditation, then to a different courtroom, and then, via a glimpse of Paul's own life, to the cross of Jesus, and finally to a shocking scene (hardly family-time television viewing) involving Paul's opponents. I doubt if the Galatians would actually have gone to sleep while listening to the letter so far, but they would certainly be wide awake after a little sequence like this.

We begin on the running track. Being a Christian is like running a race (Paul says this elsewhere, too, e.g. 1 Corinthians 9.24). The Galatians had made an excellent start. Paul isn't going to say that they have slowed down or become lazy. But someone seems to have got on the track in front of them, like a person making a political protest at an athletics meeting, and has barred their way. This 'someone' is of course the person (Paul implies in these sentences that there is one particular leader of the 'agitators' who is most responsible for what's going on) who has insisted that if they want to be full and true members of God's people they must get **circumcised**.

But this has been done through 'persuasion'. Suddenly we are in the courtroom, with clever advocates trying to persuade judge or jury that their case is right. It isn't a matter, for Paul, of people choosing one religious option or another, finding a way forward on a spiritual journey; it's a matter of truth. If it is true that the **Messiah** has died and been raised (and if that isn't true Paul knows he would be wasting his time and his life), then this in turn establishes a network of truth that carries its own persuasive power. The Galatians, however, have been persuaded for the moment, by this 'agitator', not to believe it. Don't accept that line of thought! warns Paul. This 'persuasion' is not coming from the God who called you through the **gospel** ('the one who called you' is a way of referring to God himself, as in 1.6).

Paul then leaps from the courtroom to the kitchen. Leaven is small but powerful. If you're making a loaf of bread you need leaven to make it rise, but only a few grains will do for the entire loaf. Put in those few grains, and the loaf won't be partly leavened and partly not; the leaven will work its way swiftly through the whole thing. Behind this familiar cooking image is the tradition, equally familiar to Paul, of keeping the Passover with unleavened bread, recalling the Israelites' swift departure from Egypt. Leaven was (and still is) banished altogether from Jewish kitchens at Passover time. 'Leavening the lump' became an obvious picture for compromise. Paul's point is that if the Galatians give in on this one thing, i.e. circumcision, they won't simply be all right in everything else, with one little blemish; this mistake will be like leaven, and will change everything.

Then, equally suddenly, back to the courtroom. Paul is now

playing judge and jury, and making his own decision (being 'persuaded') about the Galatians themselves, and about the person who is troubling them. He is persuaded 'in the Lord'; this probably means that, as he has wrestled with the question in prayer, he has arrived at a settled conviction that the Galatians will make up their minds the right way. But the blame will fall on the person, whoever it is, who has got them into this trouble. When Paul says 'whoever he may be', this may be a coded reference to one of the leaders in the Jerusalem church. Or he may be referring obliquely to some local leader whose name he doesn't know, or doesn't want to mention.

Another swift jump, this time to Paul's own life and work. The 'agitators' seem to have told the Galatians that Paul himself was really, like them, a 'preacher of circumcision'; it was just (they will have said) that when he was in Galatia he didn't tell them that part of the **message**, and they were completing it for him. Absolute nonsense, declares Paul. Of course, before his conversion, he would have believed that **Gentiles** had to be circumcised if they were to join God's people, but now he obviously believes no such thing. If he did, why would he still be persecuted? Suddenly there flashes on our screen the picture of Paul in his regular work. Wherever he goes he is attacked by those Jews who think he is letting the side down, who cannot bear his message of a crucified Messiah. As always in this letter, the cross is at the heart of Paul's gospel, and Paul knows it is always a 'scandal' (the word means 'something people trip over'). Of course it is: it demolishes the boast of those Jews who suppose themselves superior to the rest of humanity simply because of their ancestry.

For them, Paul has a sharp and shocking word. The agitators want to cut off the Galatians' foreskins, do they? Well, declares Paul, if they are that keen on cutting off a slice from their male body parts, why don't they go the whole way? Why don't they just castrate themselves? He says it only slightly less obviously than this (literally, 'I wish those who trouble you would have themselves cut off'). It is possible that he simply means 'I wish they would mutilate themselves' (like various pagans did in religious rituals, the best-known example being the prophets of Baal in 1 Kings 18.28). But the word in question is often used of actual castration.

This seems a violent conclusion, but Paul is probably being heavily ironic. Can't you see, he says to the Galatians, that cutting off bits of your body is neither here nor there? It's on a par with the sort of ritual markings in the flesh that various religions perform. It's on a par with castration, which was itself sometimes practised as a religious rite. But, more than that, castration of course meant preventing the man from having children. What Paul wants above all is that the people who are troubling the Galatians will lose their power, will no longer be able to dominate them or propagate their ideas among them.

If this language, and indeed the whole paragraph, seems to us quite violent and strident, that may perhaps be an indication that church people and theologians can easily become so affable, so friendly, so 'nice' to everybody that we fail to confront head-on false teachings that can do lasting damage to churches and individual Christians. Anyone who has struggled for the life and soul of a Christian community against insidious opposition will know exactly what Paul was facing. And maybe the only way we can get our message through is by vivid language, multiple imagery, not just keeping people awake but shocking them into seeing what the real issues are.

GALATIANS 5.13–21

The Law and the Spirit

[13]When God called you, my dear family, he called you to make you free. But you mustn't use that freedom as an opportunity for the flesh. Rather, you must become each other's servants, through love. [14]For the whole law is summed up in one word,

namely this: 'Love your neighbour as yourself.' [15]But if you bite each other and gobble each other up, watch out! You may end up being destroyed by each other.

[16]Let me say this to you: live by the spirit, and you won't do what the flesh wants you to. [17]For the flesh wants to go against the spirit, and the spirit against the flesh. They are opposed to each other, so that you can't do what you want. [18]But if you are led by the spirit, you are not under the law.

[19]Now the works of the flesh are obvious. They are such things as fornication, uncleanness, licentiousness, [20]idolatry, sorcery, hostilities, strife, jealousy, bursts of rage, selfish ambition, factiousness, divisions, [21]moods of envy, drunkenness, wild partying, and similar things. I told you before, and I tell you again: people who do such things will not inherit God's kingdom.

In the middle of Oxford University there stands a wonderful building, surrounded by well-kept grass. The building is a library, circular in shape, topped by a great dome. It is beautiful inside and out. People photograph it, paint it, admire it. It is called the Radcliffe Camera.

The grass that surrounds the building used to be protected with high railings – so high, in fact, that unless you were quite tall they would obscure your view of the building itself. During the Second World War, however, the government commanded that ironwork like that be taken away and melted down to make armaments. Suddenly the Radcliffe Camera, and its grass, were free from what (to judge from old pictures) was a rather forbidding barricade. During the 1950s and 1960s, there were small notices requesting people not to walk on the grass. Mostly, people obeyed.

But then, in the 1970s and 1980s, the grass became a favourite spot for tourists to picnic. People would have parties there. Less reputable characters from the town would hang out there, to drink, to beg, and sometimes to threaten passers-by.

People in the library found it was getting noisy, and they couldn't do their work. The grass was so trampled that it became worn out. The whole area no longer looked beautiful; instead, it looked messy and scruffy. Finally, in the late 1980s, the university made a decision: the railings (not so high, fortunately) had to go back. Now, once again, the grass and building are beautiful.

This little tale is all about the use and abuse of freedom. It is one thing to be set free from prison or slavery, and quite another to decide what to do with your freedom when you've got it. This is the issue faced by every criminal when released from prison: shall I use my new-found freedom to go and commit more crimes? The fact that you are, in one sense, free to walk on, and even ruin, the grass round a beautiful building doesn't mean that that is the right thing to do. Freedom *from* restraint, if it is to be of any use, must be matched by a sense of freedom *for* a particular purpose.

Paul has spent a considerable part of this letter arguing that all those who believe in Jesus **Christ** are free – free from their pagan past, but also free from the claims the Jewish **law** makes on its adherents. This is a difficult point to express clearly, because to a Jew it was precisely the law which looked after Jews, and prevented them from behaving like pagans. No, says Paul, there is a third way: a double freedom, into which you are released by the new **Exodus** which God has accomplished in Jesus the **Messiah**.

The first point he makes, then, is that freedom is *for* love. The controversies that had been raging in Galatia had apparently led to serious disturbances in the church, to which Paul refers with the strong language of 'bite' and 'devour'. It was essential that, in learning how to be truly free, the young Christians came to realize that squabbling among themselves was a sign that they were still enslaved. Worse still, it was the way to destruction. If things went on like that, quite soon there wouldn't be a church at all in Galatia.

In stressing all this, Paul quotes one of the central early Christian commandments, which is itself, of course, taken from the Old Testament: 'Love your neighbour as yourself.' If you want to keep the law, he says, this sums it all up. Jesus had said much the same (Mark 12.31). But now comes the point. The way to keep this all-embracing commandment is not by emphasizing who you are 'according to the flesh', that is, by getting **circumcised**. If you emphasize the flesh, flesh is what you'll get; and look where that will land you!

There is no suggestion that the Galatians were themselves engaged in 'the works of the flesh' that Paul lists here, in all their sordid and ugly detail. The point he is making is that if they emphasize 'the flesh', by getting circumcised, they are putting themselves on a level with the pagan world all around.

What's the alternative? The alternative is to allow the power of God's **spirit** to direct your life. If you want to fulfil the law, supremely through obeying the central command of love, this can only happen by the spirit. As so often in Paul, 'flesh' and 'spirit' are in opposition to each other. This isn't a matter of the material world against the non-material. Many of the 'works of the flesh' could be practised by a (wicked) disembodied spirit. It is, rather, a matter of where your true identity lies, where your deepest motivation comes from, and where the power that rules your life is really found.

So what is Christian freedom? It doesn't mean that, now you believe, you can do what you like. Paul is clear about that. Life is a battlefield, with flesh and spirit opposing one another, and you can never be totally off guard. What matters, though, is that your identity is that of a true child of God, indwelt by the spirit, without needing the Jewish law, and particularly its requirement of circumcision, as your badge of membership. If you're free of that, the spirit's motivation and power mean that you will also remain free from the snares of paganism, and the behaviour that goes with it. Free from the law, free from paganism, one is then free *for* God, and free to love one's neighbour. And, as the following verses will set out, one is free to be led by the spirit into a new way of life.

GALATIANS 5.22–26

Fruit of the Spirit

²²But the fruit of the spirit is love, joy, peace, great-heartedness, kindness, generosity, faithfulness, ²³gentleness, self-control. There is no law that opposes things like that! ²⁴And those who belong to the Messiah, Jesus, crucified the flesh with its passions and desires. ²⁵If we live by the spirit, let's line up with the spirit. ²⁶We shouldn't be conceited, vying with one another and jealous of each other.

The Christmas decorations were spectacular. I went down the street from store to store, and in each window – and indeed in the street itself – there were pretty lights and multicoloured decorations. Every shop seemed to have sparkling trees, alive with parcels, bells, fairies, glass balls, and all kinds of trinkets and decorations.

Or at least, they looked alive. In reality, of course, they weren't. It was all a show. I went down the same street a month later, as the decorations were being taken down. It was very bleak. The tinsel and coloured balls went back into boxes. The trees were either folded up (they weren't real, after all) or thrown out. Nothing had actually been growing on them. It looked magnificent, but it was all artificial.

If Paul is famous for his contrast of 'flesh' and '**spirit**', he is also famous for the key words he uses that go with them both. He speaks of the *works* of the 'flesh', but the *fruit* of the 'spirit'. Compare those Christmas trees for a minute with ordinary, humdrum but real fruit trees in an orchard. The Christmas trees look wonderful for a short while, but then they get packed away or thrown out. The fruit trees may not look so spectacular, but if they're properly cared for they will go on bearing fruit year after year. Which is more important? You hardly have to ask.

Underneath the two lists – the works of the flesh and the fruit of the spirit – there lies Paul's whole vision of what happens to someone when they come, through **faith** and **baptism**, into the community of the **Messiah**'s people. (Notice how, in verse 24, he speaks of Christians as 'those who belong to the Messiah'; and how he assumes, as he does in 4.4–7, that all such people are indwelt by the spirit.) There are various stages to be observed, which he condenses here.

People start off in the condition he calls 'flesh'. They are born into human families, with ethnic and territorial identities. They discover within themselves all kinds of desires, which, if allowed full rein, will produce the 'works' listed in verses 19–21. A glance back at this list will reveal that a society in which most people behaved in such a way is unlikely to be a happy or thriving place. What is more, when God finally establishes his **kingdom**, people like that will have no place in it; it would be very surprising if they did. That's not the sort of place, and state of affairs, that God wishes ultimately to create.

But then, through the announcement of the **gospel** of Jesus, God's spirit goes to work and people are renewed. The first sign of that renewal, and hence the true badge of their belonging, is their faith in Jesus as the risen Lord. But their membership in the Messiah's people involves them in a movement through death to new life (this is spelled out more fully in 2.19–20). What is left behind in this death, this co-crucifixion with the Messiah, is precisely the life in which 'the flesh' determines who one is and how one behaves.

Instead, they begin to 'bear fruit'. The nine qualities Paul lists in verses 22–23 are not things which, if we try hard enough, we could simply do without help, without the spirit. If you suspect that someone who is being kind to you is having to try very hard to do it, the kindness itself loses its flavour. The point of all of them is that when the spirit is at work they will begin to happen; new motivations will appear.

Not, of course, that this process bypasses our thinking and willing. We have to set our minds and intentions to do them; it isn't a matter of just relaxing and doing what comes naturally. Otherwise Paul wouldn't need to urge the Galatians to 'line up with the spirit' (verse 25), that is, to see the effect the spirit wants to produce, to reflect on how it will come about, and through our own moral effort to let the life of the spirit have its complete way. But the point is that when these qualities appear, with all their quiet joy, all their rich contribution to the sort of community God intends and will eventually produce, they come like the fruit in an orchard, not like the baubles on a Christmas tree. They will truly be part of who we will have become.

People of this sort, therefore, must live within their communities by the rule which flows out of this new life. Paul is still concerned here, as he was earlier in verses 13–15, that the community in Galatia, through the divisive influence of the 'agitators', was turning in angrily on itself, with some people giving themselves airs as though they were more special, more part of an inner circle or group, than the others. If the spirit is at work – and if the spirit isn't, then this is scarcely even a Christian community – then such mutual envy and rivalry must be ruled out.

Once more, then, the point he is making here is not simply that he wants them to live by the promptings of the spirit – though of course he does. The underlying point is that if they live in the way the spirit directs them to, *the Jewish **law** will have no condemnation for them* (verse 23b), and there will be no need for the disruptive effects, setting one church member against another, which the false teaching has brought about (verse 26). Thus, though this passage provides a lovely picture of what true Christian life looks like – and we might reflect that Paul could hardly write like this to them unless they knew that he had himself modelled such a spirit-filled life – its main point is still to persuade them to return to the full, complete gospel he had given them, instead of embracing the false message of the 'agitators'.

The balance this produces is as vital for the church today as it ever was. Often, today, when people emphasize the need for love, patience, gentleness and the like, this goes with an attitude to truth and the gospel which says that we shouldn't stress the things we disagree on. Equally, when people are passionate for the truth of the gospel, as Paul was, they often allow that zeal to betray them into the kind of anger and even malice that are listed under 'the works of the flesh'. Often the blend of truth and love which Paul so often urged (see, e.g., Ephesians 4.15) seems elusive in church life. Paul's own answer to the problem would be short and clear: we need to learn to line up more effectively with the spirit.

GALATIANS 6.1–5

Bearing One Another's Burdens

[1]My dear family, if someone is found out in some trespass, then you – the 'spiritual' ones! – should set such a person right, in a spirit of gentleness. Watch out for yourselves: you too may be tested. [2]Carry each other's burdens; that's the way to fulfil the Messiah's law. [3]If one of you thinks you are something when you are not, you deceive yourself. [4]Every one of you should test your own work, and then you will have reason to boast of yourself, not of someone else. [5]Each of you, you see, will have to carry your own load.

I was reading the autobiography of a world-famous cricketer. He described how for his first ten years in the game the team he played for never succeeded in winning a major trophy. They had star players, many of them of much better quality than most other teams. But they were all out for themselves, their own success, their own reputation.

After those ten years, some of the senior players retired, and a younger team, less well known, emerged. A new captain was appointed, not such a famous cricketer, but determined to pull the side together. They began to work as a team. The stars were still able to perform, but the key thing was that every single player began to work for the good of the whole. If they saw another player making a mistake they would help them instead of sneering. If someone was having a difficult patch they would encourage them instead of being glad that they could shine instead. And so on. And the miracle happened: at last, the team won the championship.

The crisis in Galatia had left the church like the first of those teams. People saw themselves as one particular 'type' of Christian, and looked down on other types. If they saw one of the others doing something wrong, they would feel smug; that, they would think, is not the way 'we' behave. At the same time, these groups were defined in terms of status, not detailed behaviour; 'we' (the Jewish Christians among them? or perhaps the richer Christians? or the ones who were Roman citizens?) were simply different because they were different. Instead of the community Paul had established, where all were equal at the foot of the cross, all equally 'in **Christ**', all equally members of Abraham's family (3.26–29), the work of the 'agitators' had left a legacy of division based on non-theological factors.

It is desperately easy for this kind of attitude to creep in to any church. Divisions in the wider society (caste, class, income, colour, the sort of home you live in) can quickly lead one group of Christians to look down on another. Often the others sneer back. What has that got to do with the **kingdom of God**?

The church is meant to work like a first-rate team. Every member should care for everyone else. Paul has just sketched out what life should be like if people are lining up with the **spirit**; now he applies this to the church's own inner life. He is careful not to accuse individual people, though there probably were some in the church who had been particularly at fault. He gives them, rather, general instructions which might be relevant to any church, and lets them work out for themselves where there was someone specific to whom it would apply.

This, too, is done with a smile in relation to the long earlier argument. You want to fulfil the **law**, do you? Very well: but let it be the law of the **Messiah**! This doesn't mean (as some have thought) that Jesus' teaching constituted a 'new law' to replace the law of Moses. To be sure, Jesus said many things about how his followers should behave. The church must take all such things utterly seriously. But the 'law' in question here is the law of love, the law of giving oneself in love and humility to the service of others. This, rather than showy behaviour which highlights one or two individuals, will be the sign that they are really 'spiritual'.

So, as Jesus the Messiah carried the cross for others, so Christians must carry one another's burdens. If my neighbour sins today, and I notice it, I must remember that it may well be me tomorrow. If it is my responsibility to help to put things right, I must do it without arrogance. If you think you are 'something', someone special, someone above the common run and rule of Christian living, able to look down on the others from a great height – why, then that attitude itself is evidence that you are not. You are deceiving yourself – but probably nobody else.

Here is the paradox of genuine community living. All for each and each for all; but one cannot slide through, hoping that other people's devotion and godliness will suffice, and that one does not need to worry about oneself. When it comes to my neighbour, I must be sure to remain humble if I offer help; when it comes to myself, I must recognize my own responsibility for my actions. 'Bear one another's burdens' (verse 2) is balanced by 'each of you must carry your own load' (verse 5).

Of course, churches are not like sports teams. They are not in competition with each other, and any suggestion of such a thing is already a step down the hill towards the unspiritual life that the Galatians were courting. But, granted that, any church that takes these verses seriously will be on the way to the only victory that counts: the victory of the cross of the Messiah, lived out in community and under the eyes of the wider world.

GALATIANS 6.6–10

Practical Support in the Church

⁶If someone is being taught the word, they should share with the teacher all the good things they have. ⁷Don't be misled; God won't have people turning their noses up at him. What you sow is what you'll reap. ⁸Yes: if you sow in the field of your flesh you will harvest decay from your flesh, but if you sow in the field of the spirit you will harvest eternal life from the spirit. ⁹Don't lose your enthusiasm for behaving properly. You'll bring in the harvest at the proper time, if you don't become weary. ¹⁰So, then, while we have the chance, let's do good to everyone, and particularly to the household of the faith.

For some years I helped to organize a fund-raising campaign for a church. It was a good cause, lots of people wanted to help, there was great enthusiasm and initiative, and eventually the money was raised. But I found it one of the hardest parts of my job.

I loved talking to people about the church and what it was doing: its worship, its life, its service to a wide community. People knew it was true, and they respected what we were doing. But when it came to suggesting that they give money, I found myself running out of words. Some people can do that easily, and I'm not one of them.

But I used to console myself by looking at how Paul went about it. The classic passage is 2 Corinthians 8 and 9, but the same thing that is true there is true here too: Paul manages to write about money without ever mentioning the word. Clearly the subject was as delicate in his world as it is in ours.

The result is the present little paragraph. Like the previous one, it has many wider applications, even though its central point is the quite specific one of financing the ministry and life of the church. Paul begins with a clear command, which most churches in the modern world studiously ignore: those who are taught the **word** should share 'in all good things' with their teacher. (By 'the word' here Paul probably means something wider than just 'the Bible', though the Bible remained at the centre of his message; he meant the whole **gospel** of Jesus, rooted in the Old Testament and worked out through the apostolic teaching.) The natural meaning of this is financial, though gifts in kind are quite appropriate as well. It is perhaps because churches have often neglected proper payment of the ministry that the ministry itself, the teaching which could and should be building up the church, has sometimes been thin and unsatisfying.

This gives quite a sharp point to the verses that follow. The picture of 'sowing' and 'harvesting' – a development in Paul's mind, perhaps, from the fruit trees at the end of chapter 5 – seems to be tied also to the giving of money. We will come to the wider meaning later, but we should pause and reflect on this.

If church members 'sow' to the **spirit**, by giving solid practical support to the church's ministry, especially in teaching and preaching, they themselves will in due course bring in a harvest. If, however, they 'sow to the flesh', spending their resources on the numerous pleasures of ordinary life, then all they will have to show for it will be the corruption and decay to which everything in the world is ultimately subject. Fine houses fall down. Splendid clothes wear out. The ministry of the word builds up people and communities, and the life they then have will gloriously outlast death itself. So Paul is eager that the ordinary Christians in Galatia should 'do good to everybody' (general phrases like this were in regular use in Paul's world, referring to financial contributions in civic and community life), especially to the family marked out by **faith**.

There is, of course, at least one important principle underneath all this. The Christian view of money is that it is a responsibility given by God. It is never purely for one's own enjoyment; it is held in trust. If used wisely ('sown', in the picture Paul is using) it will produce a harvest of good things, in terms not so much of straightforward financial investment (using money to make money – something the church at its best has always warned against) as in terms of the good things that can be done with it, things of lasting benefit to individuals and the community.

But the passage also looks wider. The contrast of 'sowing to the flesh' and 'sowing to the spirit' obviously ties in with the wider themes of the letter. 'Sowing to the flesh', in terms of the rest of Galatians, can refer to the very thing the Galatians – or some of them – were keen to do, namely, getting **circumcised**. The implication of such an act was, obviously, that one's 'flesh', and the identity which was marked by it, was the most important thing. Go that route, declares Paul, and you are on the road to ruin. The flesh will not last. Its decay and death are certain. The only harvest worth having is the one that comes from sowing to the spirit, in the wider sense of living, praying and bearing fruit in the spirit.

Then, of course, 'sowing to the flesh' can mean, in terms of 5.19–21, behaving according to the 'works of the flesh'. Here, as at each level, Christians always need the stern warning of verse 7. God won't have people turning up their noses at him; or, as some translations put it, 'God is not mocked'. This doesn't mean that God will take arbitrary vengeance on those who turn their noses up at him, who pretend that they can do what they like and get away with it. It means, more specifically, that behaviour functions like farming: God has decreed that if you sow barley, barley is what will come up, and that if you sow nettles, nettles are what will come up. This is, as we say, 'the way the world is', the way God's good creation works.

God has likewise decreed that those who 'sow' behaviour which relates to the flesh will reap the appropriate result, which is ultimately death; and that those who sow to the spirit will reap **eternal life**, the life of the new age that has already broken in, in **Christ**, and will one day be complete. Thus in the wider moral life, as well as the financial, it holds true that those who persevere with patience, not growing tired or losing their enthusiasm for living the life of the spirit, will reap the true harvest.

GALATIANS 6.11–18

Boasting in the Cross

[11]Look at the large-size letters I'm writing to you in my own hand. [12]It's the people who want to make a fine showing in the flesh who are trying to force you into getting circumcised – for this purpose only, that they may avoid persecution for the Messiah's cross. [13]You see, even the circumcised ones don't keep the law; rather, they want you to be circumcised, so that they may boast about your flesh.

[14]As for me, God forbid that I should boast – except in the cross of our Lord Jesus the Messiah, through whom the world has been crucified to me and I to the world. [15]Circumcision, you see, is nothing; neither is uncircumcision! What matters is new creation. [16]Peace and mercy on everyone who lines up by that standard – yes, on God's Israel.

[17]For the rest, let nobody make trouble for me. You see, I carry the marks of Jesus on my body.

[18]The grace of our Lord Jesus the Messiah be with your spirit, my dear family. Amen.

At least half of all the items that come through my letter-box each day are what we loosely call 'junk mail'. Often I receive letters which, though they may have my name at the top, have in fact been mass-produced by a computer as part of an advertising campaign. Even the letters that are personal, and meant for me, are often produced on a computer. They, too, can have a somewhat detached feel.

You know you are in touch with a real, living, breathing human being when your correspondent takes the trouble not only to sign his or her name but also to add a few final sentences in personal handwriting. And that is precisely what Paul does here.

He wasn't, of course, doing so at the foot of a typed letter, or one composed on a word-processor. He had been dictating to a scribe up to this point; here, following regular custom, he took the pen to write not just his name (in fact, he doesn't mention that) but his final thoughts. They are still warm and passionate; the fire has not gone out of his argument; but they have the effect of tying together several parts of the letter and bringing it to a solid and solemn conclusion. As at one or two earlier moments, when all is said and done, what matters in this controversy is the cross. And that is what he focuses on.

The cross marks the great division, not only between the church and the world, but between those in the church who are prepared to face persecution for the **Messiah** and those who aren't. The 'agitators' have been keen to mark the bodies of the Galatians with the sign that says they belong to the ethnic family of Abraham. Paul declares that the only marks that matter on his body are the wounds he has suffered as a result of his allegiance to Jesus (verse 17). If it's bodily marks you want, it is the signs of the cross, not of the circumciser's knife, that matter; and the signs of the cross are the marks of persecution, the 'wounds of Jesus'.

That, of course, is what the 'agitators' are eager to avoid. Under pressure themselves from fellow Jews to prove that they are not compromised by associating with **Gentiles**, they are passing on this pressure to the Gentile converts. But Paul can see right through their posture. He knows (as he said earlier, in 5.3) that **circumcision** only makes sense if one is going to keep the whole **law**; but the 'agitators' are only interested in this one thing, only concerned to save their own skins by cutting off other people's foreskins. They are shown up as shallow and trivial.

By contrast, Paul opens up, here in this last segment of the letter, a God's-eye view of reality which lifts our minds and hearts out beyond Galatia, out beyond the sordid details of campaigns and plots in the primitive church, and out into the rich and wide-ranging purposes of the God of love for the whole cosmos. Not only has the Messiah been crucified. Not only have Christians been crucified with him (2.19–20; 5.24). The world itself has been crucified. Calvary was the turning-point of history. The cosmos has had sentence of death passed on it – so that God's new world, God's new creation, can be born out of the old. This new creation began with Jesus himself at his **resurrection**, continues with the **spirit**-given new life which wells up in all those who belong to the Messiah, and will go on until, as Paul says in Romans 8, the whole creation will be set free from its own slavery and will share the freedom of the glory of God's children.

This, then, is at the heart of everything for Paul, and this is what drives his thought throughout Galatians. With the cross of Jesus the old world is born and the new one is promised. How then can anyone who has glimpsed Jesus as the crucified Messiah want to cling to the values, the identity-markers, the way of life of the world that has already been pronounced dead on the cross? What matters is neither circumcision nor uncircumcision – neither the marks in the flesh of the Jew nor the absence of such marks in the Gentile. What matters is that God has unleashed upon the world his own new creation, and through the **gospel** of Jesus invites all to share equally in its blessings, its new life, its promises for the future.

Those who respond in **faith** are thus given the title of great honour: they are (verse 16) 'the Israel of God'. They are, after all, Abraham's family (chapter 3); they are the Isaac-family rather than the Ishmael-one (chapter 4); they fulfil the whole law in their love for one another (chapter 5). They are God's chosen people.

Of course, we should remember that, when Paul was writing, the majority of Christians were Jews by birth. We should not allow our reading of him to suggest, as some have tragically done, that God has turned his back on the Jews and has allowed a Gentile community to take over instead. That is what Paul sets his face against in (for instance) Romans 9—11. But we should not allow our awareness of that problem to prevent us seeing and feeling the force of what he says here. The Galatians – and all who believe in Jesus – are now God's Israel, God's light to his world, called to get in line with the measuring-rod of the new creation, to share God's peace and mercy and to bring it to his world.

The final lines of the letter are a benediction not only on the Galatians but on all of us who read these words. It is all of grace from start to finish: the grace of our Lord Jesus, the Messiah. God, in the Messiah, took the initiative in the plan of salvation; like Paul's apostleship itself (chapter 1), the gospel does not come from human sources, and membership in the Messiah's people is not defined by human categories. Grace reaches out and embraces the whole world. The sign of that embrace is not a mark in the flesh, but the presence and joy of the spirit. So it was in the first century; so it is now, in the church and world that still needs the message of Galatians. So it will be until faith is rewarded with sight, patience with the final harvest, and eager hope with fulfilment.

1 THESSALONIANS

1 THESSALONIANS 1.1–5

The Gospel Comes to Thessalonica

¹Paul, Silvanus and Timothy, to the community of Thessalonians in God the father and the Lord Jesus, the Messiah. Grace to you and peace.

²We always give thanks to God for all of you, as we make mention of you in our prayers. ³We constantly remember the accomplishment of your faith, the hard work of your love, and the patience of your hope in our Lord Jesus Christ, in the presence of God our father.

⁴Dear family, beloved by God, we know that God has chosen you; ⁵because our gospel didn't come to you in word only, but in power, and in the holy spirit, and in great assurance. You know what sort of people we turned out to be, for your sake, when we were among you.

I hesitated long over the decision. I had to make up my mind whether to admit to the university a student whose grades were not quite as high as we would normally require. She was clearly intelligent, and capable of hard work, but why were some of the grades just a little bit lower than we had expected? Then I thought back to the interview my colleagues and I had had with the student. She had come alive. She was clearly not only interested in the subject, but enthusiastic, and able to take in new ideas and make them her own. Remembering those first impressions vividly, I made the decision. We would admit her to the college. Three years later I was vindicated: she graduated with top honours.

Paul vividly remembers his first impressions of the Thessalonian Christians to whom he writes this letter. Thessalonica – modern Thessaloniki, or Salonica – was, and is, a thriving seaport in northern Greece, roughly 200 miles north of Athens. Paul had come there after preaching in Philippi, further east, where he had been beaten and thrown in prison before pointing out that he was a Roman citizen. The story of that journey is told in Acts 16 and 17.

Though Paul's normal practice was to begin his preaching in the Jewish synagogue or place of prayer, it seems that most of the people who came to believe his **message** were non-Jews. For them, there was a double barrier to be crossed before they could accept the **gospel**. It was not only a crazy message about a man who was dead and then came to life again. It was a crazy *Jewish* message. Paul must have known, as he went from place to place, that most people who heard what he was talking about were bound to think him mad.

And yet these people had not. Some in Thessalonica, as in most places he went, found that something happened to them when they listened to his message. A strange power gripped them – the power that, Paul would tell them, was the **holy spirit** at work. They would suddenly understand what he was saying. It would grasp their hearts and minds. Paul and his companions, explaining the gospel to them, would become excited as they saw the message take hold, make sense, and begin its work of transforming hearts and lives. That memory lingered on even though Paul, Silvanus and Timothy had moved south, to Beroea, Athens and now Corinth (Paul doesn't say so in the letter, but it is likely that he was writing this from Corinth, where he stayed for over two years).

So when he looks back and gives thanks to God for them he knows that God was indeed at work in them as the word of the gospel was preached. His vivid memory of those early days, of their response and strong conviction, was clear proof that God had chosen them (verse 4). They had not come to **faith** by accident. God wanted them to be his beachhead into that part of northern Greece, a beacon of light to illuminate the world around. Though, as we shall see, Paul nursed anxieties about how they were getting on in their faith and life, his bedrock conviction was that God had taken the initiative in grasping them with the gospel.

This is the centre of Paul's opening thanksgiving. Like most of his letters, this one starts with him telling his readers how he prays for them – a remarkable pastoral move in itself. Writing with his companions Silvanus (the 'Silas' of Acts 15.27, etc.) and Timothy, his young assistant, Paul knows he can address the Christians in Thessalonica as 'the community in God the father and the Lord Jesus the **Messiah**'. The word for 'community' is sometimes translated 'church', but it was a common word for a gathering or assembly. What distinguished this community from others was that it was not only located in a particular place, but 'in' a particular god – the god who is in fact God, the one true God, known to Jews and Christians as father, and known now in the gospel as the one who sent Jesus to be Messiah and so Lord of the world. As so often with Paul, his opening words and phrases contain, in a nutshell, a good deal that he will spell out later in the letter.

His opening thanksgiving and prayer actually extend, in a rambling sort of way, for over half the letter – to the end of chapter 3, in fact; and there is probably a good reason for this. The church in Thessalonica is very young, probably not more than a few months old. Already they have faced great difficulties; they have been persecuted, and some of them have died (whether from the persecution or from other causes, Paul does not say). By way of rooting them the more firmly in the gospel, Paul reminds them at length of what happened when he arrived and preached there; of the example he and his companions set them; of Timothy's recent visit and the good report he had brought back. And he does all this within the broad framework of telling them how they feature in his prayers, which they do constantly (verse 2).

In particular, he recalls how, even in the short time he spent with them after the initial preaching, they already demonstrated three things which he saw as signs of life. Faith, love and hope: Paul uses this threesome elsewhere, particularly in 1 Corinthians 13.13, but clearly it was a regular part of his thinking and teaching about basic Christian living.

Each one demands effort. Faith is something you have to

work at. It is not a 'work' in the sense of a 'work of the **law**' done to earn favour with God, but a work of love, done out of gratitude for grace. It means thinking the gospel through, and bringing our minds and wills into line with it. Love – which, as Paul will show later in the letter (4.9–12), is a very practical thing – also requires the kind of effort we associate with hard physical work. Hope needs patience, which is also demanding.

The Thessalonians had all three. Could the same be said for your church?

1 THESSALONIANS 1.6–10

The Thessalonians' Faith

> [6]And you learned how to copy us – and the Lord! When you received the word, you had a lot to suffer, but you also had the holy spirit's joy. [7]As a result, you became a model for all the believers in both Macedonia and Achaea. [8]For the word of the Lord has resonated out from you, not only in Macedonia and Achaea; your faith in God has gone out to people everywhere. This means that we haven't had to say anything. [9]They themselves tell the story of the kind of welcome we had from you, and how you turned to God from idols, to serve the living and true God, [10]and to wait for his son from heaven, whom he raised from the dead – Jesus, who delivers us from the coming fury.

'Well,' I said last week when my son came home from a movie, 'did you enjoy it?'

I knew the answer as I asked the question. The movie was OK, but not that great. If he'd really enjoyed it, I wouldn't have had to ask. He would have come bounding in through the front door, eager to tell me about it.

There are some experiences which are so remarkable that you just have to talk to someone about them. Sometimes you hear a piece of music, read a book, watch a movie, or witness a scene which is so striking that you can't help yourself. As soon as you meet someone you can tell, you say, 'I must tell you about the movie . . .' or whatever it is. Then it's clear that it really has made an impression.

What happened when Paul and his companions arrived in Thessalonica made that sort of impression, not only on the people who heard and believed the **gospel**, but on people of all sorts, all around Greece and the neighbouring countries. Nobody had to say, 'Have you heard about those peculiar Jews who are going around talking about someone called Jesus?' because everybody who had heard about them was telling someone else without being asked. That's the meaning of what Paul says here: the message was echoing around north and south Greece (Macedonia in the north, Achaea in the south), and everywhere else as well – presumably Asia and Bithynia (modern Turkey) to the east and Illyricum, Moesia and the other small Balkan countries to the north.

What people were talking about particularly was not just the new church, but the way it had come into being. In this passage and the following one Paul rejoices in the welcome that had been given to him and his companions, and more especially to the message they were bringing. The remarkable thing was the instant effect the gospel had had. At the heart of it – and this is never far from Paul's mind throughout the letter – was the call to worship the true God rather than idols.

That was simply unheard of in Paul's world. It would be like asking people in a modern city to give up using motor cars, computers and telephones. The gods of Greek and Roman paganism were everywhere. If you were going to plant a tree, you would pray to the relevant god. If you were going on a business trip, a quick visit to the appropriate shrine was in order. If you or your son or daughter was getting married, serious and costly worship of the relevant deity was expected. At every turn in the road the gods were there: unpredictable, possibly malevolent, sometimes at war among themselves, so that you could never do too much in the way of placating them, making sure you'd got them on your side.

In particular – and this will be important later on in the letter – there was one recent arrival among the gods of Greece and Rome. When Augustus defeated his rivals and became emperor of Rome and its enormous subject lands, he declared that his adopted father, Julius Caesar, had become a god. When Augustus himself died in AD 14, his successor, Tiberius, did the same for him. Augustus during his lifetime, and Tiberius during his, were thus styled 'son of the god'. Before too long, however, especially in the eastern Mediterranean areas where people were quite used to worshipping rulers, folk had got the message and had begun to worship the present emperor, not just the previous one. It seemed safer, and equally logical. Anyone who could rule most of the world that people knew then, and keep it in peace and prosperity, must (so it was widely thought) have something divine about them. The city of Rome was itself deified; shrines to 'Rome and the Emperor' sprang up as local magistrates and rulers were keen to demonstrate their political loyalty. Cities tumbled over themselves to build temples for these new divinities.

Into this world came three unknown Jews, telling pagans that there was one true God (other Jews had done that) and that this God had a true son, and had demonstrated this fact by raising him from the dead (nobody had ever said that before). And people in Thessalonica, knowing from the start the risk they would be taking, turned away from their idols to this living God, and discovered, at the same moment, suffering and joy (verse 6). That is what conversion is all about: the word 'turned' in verse 9 is as close as Paul gets to a technical term for conversion itself, what happens when someone stops going in one direction, turns around and begins going the other way.

Discovering the living God, and his son alive after death, also put the Thessalonian Christians on the track of the characteristically Christian hope, something Paul will say more about later in the letter. They were to wait for Jesus to appear from **heaven**. There would come a time of great distress, a time for which the only word would be 'wrath' or 'fury', the strange and dark reaction of a loving and holy God to all that distorts and defaces his world. (People sometimes ask how a loving God can also be angry. Looking back at the inhumane and brutal twentieth century, one has to say that a good and loving God *must* be angry when faced with such wickedness.) But, though this time of wrath will surely come, Jesus himself will deliver his people from it. That was central to the Christian hope in the first century, and remains central today.

The Thessalonian Christians had only been believers for a short time; we don't know how long, but it can't have been more than a year or so at the outside. But already people for hundreds of miles around were talking about this unheard-of thing: quite ordinary people had done something extraordinary, in response to an unexpected message. The only explanation was that the living God had been at work through the gospel message about Jesus. And the only appropriate response to that is thanksgiving and celebration. This first chapter of the letter is Paul's way of saying 'thank you' to God for the Thessalonians, and of encouraging them as well by telling them he's doing so.

1 THESSALONIANS 2.1–8

Paul's Ministry in Thessalonica

¹For you yourselves know, my dear family, that the welcome we had from you didn't turn out to be empty. ²On the contrary. We had already undergone awful things and been shamefully treated in Philippi, as you know; but we were open and exuberant in our God in declaring to you the gospel of God, despite a good deal of opposition.

³When we make our appeal, you see, we are not deceiving people. We don't have any impure motives; we aren't playing some kind of trick. ⁴Rather, we speak as people whom God has validated to be entrusted with the gospel; not with a view to

pleasing people, but in order to please God, who validates our hearts.

5For we never used flattering words, as you know. Nor were we saying things insincerely, as a cover-up for greed, as God is our witness. 6We weren't looking for recognition from anybody, either you or anyone else – 7though we could have imposed on you, as the Messiah's emissaries. But we were gentle among you, like a nurse taking care of her own children. 8We were so devoted to you that we gladly intend to share with you not only the gospel of God but our own lives, because you became so dear to us.

The ancient world, like the modern one, learned to be cynical about almost everything. If a letter arrives offering me a wonderful free gift, I know it's a trap to lure me into paying for something I don't really want. If someone offers to do something wonderfully kind for you, you all too easily ask what's in it for them. When a holiday company invites me for a free weekend in one of their vacation homes, I know they are hoping I will want to rent one on a permanent basis. And so on.

The ancient world had its fair share of wandering salesmen, travelling teachers, people who tried to make a living by offering their hearers fresh wisdom or insight, some kind of magic, a new philosophy, or whatever. When Paul and his companions arrived in a city and began to tell their strange story, many people must have thought that's the sort of people they were. The knowing ones in the crowd would be waiting for the moment when the speakers produced a money-bag and requested contributions, or invited people to pay to hear more in private. The cynical ones among them would be waiting for darker events still: for the speakers to single out for special private 'instruction' those (of either sex) who were physically attractive. At the very least, it would be expected that newly arrived teachers would want to make a good name for themselves, to be well known and well liked around the town.

Paul knows that, if anyone tried to charge him with such trickery, the Thessalonians would refute it all. In a passage that ought to be written out in large letters and hanging on the wall in every Christian minister's house – or, perhaps better, engraved in letters of gold on his or her heart – Paul reminds them that his arrival in Thessalonica, and his pattern of life while there, had nothing in common with the kind of tricks people would have expected. His understanding of his own task and role was completely different. It's worth looking at it closely, step by step. (We note that Paul says 'we' rather than 'I' throughout; Silvanus and Timothy are included in the description, but there is no doubt that it's Paul's thinking that lies behind it all.)

It had begun with his own suffering. If someone does something and gets paid handsomely for it, the next time they do it we can assume that part of the reason is the money. But if they do something and find themselves beaten up and thrown into jail, the next time they do it we rightly assume that they have some reason so compelling that it will make them carry on even though they run the same risk. So it was with Paul; he arrived in Thessalonica with the physical and emotional scars of his shameful treatment in Philippi, and when he spoke this time there was once again much opposition. But, so far from being cowed, or afraid that the same thing might happen, Paul carried right on, and indeed found himself speaking with great freedom and excitement; the key word in verse 2 indicates that he was bold, outspoken, fearless in telling the whole **gospel**. As he himself says frequently, somehow the suffering not only validates the gospel (it shows that the preacher isn't in it for the wrong reasons), but also, surprisingly, gives a sense of joy and freedom. Clearly the world-shaking message is going home.

At the heart of it all is the approval, not of humans, but of God. Again and again in this passage Paul speaks of God: he was bold in God (verse 2a), he preached the gospel of God (verses 2b, 8), he had been approved or validated by God (verse 4a), he was aiming simply to please God (verse 4b), and God was his witness that he was not exercising this ministry in secret pursuit of greed (verse 5). Having spoken of the true and living God in contrast to idols (1.9), it's clear that Paul found himself living in the presence of that God, knowing that his own heart was under scrutiny as he went about his work. God had entrusted him with the gospel (verse 4), like a monarch entrusting to a messenger an announcement for subjects far away. His responsibility was to deliver the message whole and entire, without regard for his own place in the proceedings, or to any honour or reward that might or might not come his way. He wasn't going to allow his status as a herald of the king to puff up his own self-importance.

In his dealings with the Thessalonians themselves, as a result, Paul could afford to be gentle, caring and loving. He wasn't secretly out to gain anything from them; he simply and genuinely wanted the love of God to embrace them, and as he worked among them he found that his own love was drawn out to them as well. Those who have had the privilege of being ministered to by people with this motivation know how wonderful it is when pastors share with them not only the gospel but their own very selves. Those of us who have had good Christian friends, at school, college, work or in social life, will know the same thing.

And, in case anyone supposes (if we find ourselves being cynical as we read Paul) that Paul is praising himself too much, we should reflect that he could hardly have written all this – and the scribe taking Paul's dictation could hardly have copied it down – if it wasn't true. The Thessalonians would recognize this self-portrait when they heard the letter. The question for all Christian ministers is: if we were to describe ourselves like this, would anyone recognize who we were talking about?

1 THESSALONIANS 2.9–12
Paul's Fatherly Concern

⁹My dear family, you will recall our hard toil, our labour. We worked night and day so as not to be a burden to any of you while we announced to you the gospel of God. ¹⁰You are witnesses, and so is God, of our holy, upright and blameless behaviour towards you believers. ¹¹You know how, like a father to his own children, ¹²we encouraged each of you, and strengthened you, and made it clear to you that you should behave in a manner worthy of the God who calls you into his own kingdom and glory.

Perhaps the most remarkable thing about Paul's missionary work is that when he arrived in a new town the people there had quite literally never seen anything of the sort before. They had seen other travelling teachers, but none like this. They knew of religious leaders; they knew of ethnic groups (such as the Jews) who had their own religion and sometimes welcomed outsiders; but none of them had behaved as Paul did. They had no idea that this sort of lifestyle was possible, let alone desirable.

It was, we may assume, an equally remarkable challenge for Paul himself: that he should be the principal model for his new converts, and should teach them by example what sort of a life would bring glory to the living God he was telling them about. We may assume that by the time he arrived in Thessalonica he had already thought through what it would mean, and knew exactly what needed to be done.

The first thing concerned money. He has already made the point in verse 7 that, as an **apostle** of **Christ** – in other words, as an ambassador of the world's true king! – he could with complete justification have requested financial support. As the Corinthian correspondence makes clear, he was treading a fine line at this point: if he accepted money from the churches where he was working, people might accuse him of working only for pay; but, if he didn't take money, people might accuse him of not really 'belonging' to them. And it's clear that he expects the normal ministry within churches themselves, as opposed to his work as their initial apostle and evangelist, to be properly paid (e.g., Galatians 6.6; 1 Timothy 5.17–18). But he has settled it as his own practice that he will work with his own hands to earn what he needs while he engages in primary evangelism and teaching.

We know from Acts what Paul did for a living: he made tents (Acts 18.3; 20.34; cf. 1 Corinthians 4.12). This involved hard physical work, cutting, tooling and stitching leather. We must presume that Paul would have worked either in the home he was renting, or in a separate workshop where he could be closer to his potential customers. He would thus need to pay at least one regular rent, as well as buying food and materials. He would be in daily contact with all kinds of people, and his integrity as a producer of worthwhile goods and as a man of business would be under regular public scrutiny. His preaching and teaching, though he would doubtless carry on innumerable conversations while at work, would be fitted in on the **sabbath**, and in the odd spare hours in the evenings, before returning to finish a tent he was working on while others were relaxing, drinking, and preparing for sleep. This must have made quite an impression, but Paul didn't do it for show; he did it because he intended the new Christians to know that he was there for them like a father for his children. Fathers don't charge their children for bringing them up, for raising them to be the people they ought to be.

That was what Paul's work was about. The **gospel** itself – the summons to worship the God now revealed in Jesus the **Messiah** – involved the call to seek and find God's **kingdom** and glory; and the way to that goal was the way of holiness. The description of the goal in verse 12, and of Paul's efforts to make clear the way to it, are so striking – a typical example of

Paul rounding off a train of thought with a deep and rich statement – that it's worth looking at it in detail.

The central thing he wants them to do is, literally, to 'walk worthy of God'. The word 'walk' is a regular Pauline word for 'behaviour', following the standard use of the equivalent Hebrew word. Behaviour is seen as a matter of putting one foot in front of another; good behaviour is taking care with the direction and placing of those feet.

Most of the gods the Thessalonians had known before would have made certain requirements on them, mostly to do with the kind of worship they expected rather than details of daily behaviour. But the most recent god to be proclaimed in Greece, namely Caesar himself, already possessed a kingdom and glory, and expected his subjects to express their loyalty to him in all possible ways. Paul knows quite well that his gospel proclaims the true God, the true kingdom and the true glory, and that this kingdom and glory are not things God intends to keep to himself but rather things he wants to share with all his people.

But the way to this kingdom and glory, the way which begins with **faith** in this one God (1.9), must continue with a complete lifestyle that is worthy of this same living God. As Caesar's kingship extended throughout the whole worldwide empire, so God's kingship extends to every corner of human life: not because God is a snooping, prying God, but because humans are made in his image, designed to reflect his glory with every facet of their personality. Christian behaviour is not, then, a matter of a few rules made up by a heavenly bureaucrat or policeman, but a matter of reflecting God's glory with every part of life.

This is itself such a novel and demanding idea that Paul had to spell it out and encourage it from every possible angle. He exhorted them like a sports coach telling his team how to win; he encouraged them like a friend strengthening someone facing a daunting task; he testified to them like a witness in a court of law. He lost no opportunity to explain to them that the living God wanted living human beings to reflect his glory, and that he had called them, summoned them, bidden them to this utterly demanding, but utterly rewarding, way of life.

But he didn't just use words. The whole point of 2.1–12 is that Paul was telling them all this by his own example. Several years ago, in a church in Scotland, I heard a preacher quoting an old poem which sums this up exactly. I don't know who wrote it, but they might have been reading 1 Thessalonians. This is exactly what Paul is talking about.

> I'd rather see a sermon than hear one, any day;
> I'd rather one would walk with me than merely show
>   the way.
> The eye's a better pupil, more willing than the ear;
> Fine counsel is confusing, but example's always clear.

1 THESSALONIANS 2.13–16

The Persecuted Church

[13]So, therefore, we thank God constantly that when you received the word of God which you heard from us, you accepted it, not as the word of men but – as it really is! – the word of God which is at work in you believers. [14]For, my dear family, you came to copy God's communities in Judaea in the Messiah, Jesus. You suffered the same things from your own people as they did from the Judaeans. [15]It was the Judaeans, you see, who killed the Lord Jesus and the prophets, and who expelled us. They displease God; they are opposing all people; [16]they forbid us to speak to the Gentiles so that they may be saved. This has had the effect of completing the full total of their sins. But the fury has come upon them for good.

The day started clear and bright, with not a cloud in the sky. My son and I set off to climb in the mountains with every hope that the weather would hold. But as we reached the top of our first peak, a shock awaited us. We were climbing steeply on the south side, and couldn't see the sky to the north; but when we came up on the summit ridge, we saw the sky darkening dangerously, with thick black clouds coming straight towards us on a strong wind. We quickly put on our protective clothing. Within 20 minutes the whole sky was black. A few minutes later, the rain was sweeping down all around us, and hardly stopped for the rest of the day.

That is the feeling we get at this point in the letter. If somebody had cut off 1 Thessalonians at verse 13 of chapter 2, we would have a sense of clear skies, beautiful views, and everything in the young church developing straightforwardly. Alas, things are not usually like that in the **kingdom of God** in its present form. There is a struggle still going on, and those who give their allegiance to Jesus as **Messiah** and Lord will become involved in it whether they like it or not.

Paul's own struggles have been clear from early on. He had been beaten and imprisoned in Philippi, and there was much opposition when he worked in Thessalonica itself (2.2). But now we hear that the Thessalonians, too, have already suffered for their new-found **faith**. Indeed, Paul gives this as the reason, at least in part, why he can tell that the **gospel** of Jesus had had its effect in them, not as a mere human message but as the word of God himself.

If it had been a merely human message, one might expect that when the hearers began to be persecuted for accepting it they would turn back and give it up. But they have not. The word has produced in them the same kind of steadfastness as that of the very first Christians, the communities of Jesus' followers in Judaea. (As in 1.1, the word sometimes translated 'church' is more general, meaning 'community' or 'assembly'. 'God's communities in Judaea' by itself could mean simply the Jewish synagogues; so Paul adds 'in the Messiah, Jesus'.) Their suffering, in other words, doesn't mean that something has gone badly wrong with God's purpose for them; it means that they are on the same map as the very first churches. They are on the same map, too, as Paul himself.

The dark cloud of suffering hangs over much of the early Christian experience. Why? What is the wind that brings it on?

Paul would have said, without a doubt, that it was because the church, in giving its allegiance to the crucified Jesus as Lord, was challenging the still-active powers of the world. The battle between the true God and the powers of evil that enslave and deface humankind came to its height on the cross. But the church is charged with implementing the victory that was won there, and the powers don't like it.

At the wider level, this means that pagan rulers and author-ities, and supremely Caesar himself, will strongly object to the gospel of 'another king' being announced within their domains (this, according to Acts 17.7, is precisely what happened when Paul was first at Thessalonica). At the more focused level, it meant that those Judaeans who had rejected the message of Jesus, which challenged their whole view of God, the world and themselves, had continued to reject the deeply subversive claims of the early Jewish Christians in their midst, and had indeed done their best to stamp out the little movement. Paul should know; he had been one of the persecutors himself (see Galatians 1.13–14).

It is important to realize that when he says 'Judaeans' here in verse 14 he doesn't simply mean 'the Jews'. He was himself a Jew, as were all the first Christians. But Paul knows, because he was part of the movement himself, that within Judaea many Jews had been bitterly opposed not only to Jesus, resulting in their authorities handing him over to the Romans for crucifixion, but also to the groups that sprang up after his **resurrection**, hailing him as Messiah and Lord. Paul, in line with what he says elsewhere (e.g. Romans 9.6—10.4), connects this rejection of God's Messiah with his fellow Jews' much earlier rejection of the prophets. He declares, not least on the evidence of what had happened in Galatia, that the Jews who did not believe in

Jesus seemed bent on preventing a **Gentile** mission taking place at all. Believing passionately that God's salvation was for them only, they regarded as blasphemous the message of a crucified Messiah who offered salvation on equal terms to Gentiles as well.

To explain this Paul draws, in a typically brief turn of phrase, on the biblical idea of God's wrath or fury. God's anger is never capricious or malevolent; when humans reject him, and behave in ways that undermine his wise and generous designs for them and the world, he does not instantly punish, but allows space for **repentance**. If this does not happen, though, wickedness builds up, sin accumulates, until the point where God must say 'enough' and bring things to an end. This, according to Genesis 15.16, is what happened with the Canaanites, and explains the long time Israel had to spend in Egypt. Paul sees the people of Judaea now in the same position: courting disaster by continuing to oppose the gospel.

The result will be, as the whole first Christian generation knew, the one that Jesus himself had prophesied: the city and **Temple** would be destroyed. Matthew, Mark and particularly Luke make this a major theme in their accounts of Jesus' preaching. Paul, writing to the Thessalonians 20 years or so after the crucifixion, knows that there cannot be much more time before it happens. Jesus had said it would take place within a generation (Mark 13.30), and all the signs were that it would not be long delayed. Though Paul himself did not live to hear of it, had he been alive in AD 70 he would undoubtedly have declared that the events of that year were indeed the outpouring of God's wrath. That, after all, was the verdict of the Jewish historian Josephus as well.

This doesn't mean that God had finished with the Jews as a people. Paul addresses that issue quite fully in Romans 9—11, and reaches a very different conclusion. It does mean that the present opposition suffered by the Christian Jews in Judaea from their non-Christian neighbours would result in vindication.

Paul holds out the same promise to the Christian Gentiles in Thessalonica: they, presently suffering at the hands of their own countrymen, will in the end be vindicated.

It is a solemn and serious passage. But it speaks volumes to those – and there are many – who are persecuted even today for their faith in Jesus. This does not mean that something has gone badly wrong with God's plan; merely that they are sharing the sufferings of Christ, and will like him be vindicated in God's good time.

1 THESSALONIANS 2.17–20

Paul's Joy and Crown

[17]As for us, my dear family, we were snatched away from you for a short time, in person though not in heart. We longed eagerly, with a great desire, to see you face to face. [18]That's why we wanted to come to you – I, Paul, again and again – but the satan got in our way.

[19]Don't you see? When our Lord Jesus is present once more, what is my hope, my joy, the crown of my boasting before him? It's you! [20]Yes: you are our glory and our joy.

There were tear-jerking scenes on the television last night. Twin baby girls had been adopted by a couple from another country, who had found the children being advertised for adoption over the Internet. But another couple, from the children's own country, thought the twins had been promised to them. Meanwhile the children's natural mother changed her mind and said she wanted them back. Then, apparently to protect the babies from any more exposure to the bright lights of the media, officials from the government's social agency took the children away for their own protection, and gave them into the care of foster parents. It was a legal, moral and emotional nightmare for all concerned.

For a little baby, to be taken away from a parent is often

traumatic – though, in the televised case, the babies seemed to be the least upset of all the people involved. For a parent, to have a child taken away is agony. Even in the animal kingdom, the mother will often make a great fuss about losing a baby; how much more in the human world.

That is the image Paul uses for how he felt about having to leave the Thessalonians, once his presence in their city looked like precipitating another riot. These verses, and the whole of the next chapter, grow out of his sense of deep bonding with them, like a mother with the baby she has begun to feed. He has been snatched away from them, and his whole heart and being yearns to be face to face with them again. This entire section, from 1.2 right through to 3.13, is framed by thanksgiving and prayer, and Paul here expresses his deepest emotions in the presence of God. Any idea that he was a cerebral theologian only, organizing his ideas into neat patterns without being caught up in the power and glory, and the emotional ties, of the **gospel**, is completely ruled out by this passage.

Like an anxious parent, Paul's every thought has been how to get back to see his beloved (and, he fears, endangered) children again. As he journeys south, to Beroea, Athens and then Corinth, at every turn he is trying to work out ways of going back north to them once more. But, he says, '**the satan** got in our way.' He says something similar in Romans 1.13, about his unfulfilled desire to go to Rome. What does he mean?

Paul doesn't often mention 'the satan', but when he does he seems to be aware that behind at least some of the ordinary frustrations and thwarted plans that are common to the human race we may discern a darker and more malevolent force at work. This force – it may be going too far to see it as 'personal' – embodies itself from time to time in human beings and organizations that block God's purpose or hold it up for a while. In the present case, Paul presumably means that the death-threats he was receiving as he journeyed south made it quite impossible for him to return to northern Greece again just at the moment. In particular, they thwarted his deeply pastoral purpose, to care for the new little church, to teach them the way of holiness, and to bring them the comfort that a fuller understanding of the gospel would afford.

But of course if Paul had always been with his churches we would never have had his letters. His letters are a substitute for his personal presence, binding him and the churches together in a fellowship which, though not face to face as they would have liked, is nevertheless a fellowship of heart and mind. Underneath the opposition of 'the satan' we may sometimes discern the strange providence of God. This does not rob the 'satanic' opposition of danger or threat, but reminds us that God remains sovereign even over present dark frustrations.

Paul's reason for longing to see them is not simply that they have become very dear to him. It also has a forward look. From this point on the letter increasingly looks ahead to the great coming day, the day when Jesus will be revealed once more and so will be personally present with his people, and as Lord of the world. We shall have more to say about this when we reach 4.13–18. But for the moment we note that when Paul looks forward to that day, as he does eagerly, the thing that he regards as his reason for confidence, his 'boasting', in the presence of the Lord is the Christians who have become established and mature through his work. They are his 'hope, joy and crown', his 'glory and joy'.

This is remarkable for several reasons, and should be an encouragement and stimulus both to pastors and to congregations. But it might, at first glance, seem to be odd. Surely for Paul the single hope for the future, the thing that will stand him in good stead on the last day, is simply the cross and **resurrection** of Jesus Christ? 'God forbid', he writes in Galatians 6.14, 'that I should boast, except in the cross of our Lord Jesus the **Messiah.**' Has he changed his mind?

Of course not. Jesus' death and resurrection remain foundational for who Paul is and what he does (see, e.g. 1 Thessalonians

4.14). But the 'boasting' he there refers to relates to his *present status*, his standing before God in **faith**; this is what rules out, as Galatians makes clear, all present standing based on the marks of belonging to a particular race or tribe, or on any human achievement or effort. What Paul is now talking about is his hope for the future, for the last day when, as he says in Galatians 5.6, what will count is 'faith at work through love'. For Paul, the work of love has meant the founding and nurturing of churches, as the substantial sign that the living God has indeed been at work through him.

Of course, there are thousands of different Christian callings, most of them not nearly so spectacular and obvious as Paul's. Each of us has our own work of love to perform, whether it be quiet and secret or well known and public. Each pastor and teacher should look to the future, and see those in their charge as their potential joy, hope and crown. And each congregation should recognize that this is how they will appear on the last day. Both should be challenged and encouraged, by this forward look, to learn and live the faith, to celebrate the hope, to consolidate and practise the love revealed in the gospel.

1 THESSALONIANS 3.1–5

The Sending of Timothy

[1]So, when it got to the point that we couldn't bear it any longer, Silvanus and I decided to remain in Athens by ourselves, [2]and we sent Timothy – our brother, and God's fellow-worker in the gospel of the Messiah – so that he could strengthen you and bring comfort to your faith, [3]so that you wouldn't be pulled off course by these sufferings. You yourselves know, don't you, that this is what we are bound to face. [4]For when we were with you, we told you ahead of time that we would undergo suffering; that's how it has turned out, and you know about it. [5]That's why, when I too couldn't bear it any longer, I sent Timothy, so that I could find out about your

faithfulness, in case somehow the tempter had put you to the test and our work would be in ruins.

The young adult daughter of some friends of ours went on a trip round the world, and was so enjoying life that, at one stage, she didn't phone home for several weeks. Her parents had no way of getting in touch, and were beside themselves with worry. At last the local church held a prayer meeting to ask for God's help. The next day the girl phoned up, happy and unconcerned.

Parents lie awake at night and worry about their children. This is how it has always been, and we may assume that it's part of normal human life. Often children don't realize how much the parents are thinking about them, concerned for their welfare, turning over in their minds all the things that might happen to them. Sometimes Christian teachers – including Jesus himself (Matthew 6.25–34), and Paul too (Philippians 4.6) – tell us not to have anxieties about anything. There is, to be sure, a morbid, depressed sort of anxiety that fails to trust God at all; that is of course to be resisted. But where we have a responsibility for someone, it is right and natural to be anxious, and to allow that anxiety appropriate expression. Thus it was with Paul as, in Athens with Silvanus and Timothy, his thoughts about the Thessalonians overflowed and he felt obliged to send Timothy to find out how they were getting on.

This chapter tells us, in fact, one of the main reasons for Paul's writing this letter. Timothy has returned from them with good news. Yes, they are suffering; but no, this hasn't made them give up the **faith**, and in fact they are in excellent heart, as we shall see. They have some questions; Timothy has told Paul that there are one or two things they need further teaching about, and Paul will get to that in chapters 4 and 5. But at the moment he is explaining his anxieties, and it's worth looking closely at them to see what it is that a great and loving pastor rightly fears in respect of the flock.

Paul's basic fear is that they may have been swept off track, like a ship blown away from its proper course, or like someone lured away from their proper path by enticing words. Paul may mean that their sufferings themselves are the force that could distract them; or perhaps that, in the midst of these sufferings, people near and dear to them will begin to suggest that, if only they compromised a bit on their extraordinary allegiance to Jesus, they wouldn't have to undergo such things.

Either way, the key word that brings into focus the feature of their life which is at risk is the word in verses 2 and 5 sometimes translated 'faith', but also meaning 'faithfulness' or 'loyalty' or 'allegiance'. All these meanings seem to be operating simultaneously. What Paul is afraid of is compromise, of them abandoning their firm hold on the **gospel**, their unswerving loyalty to their new-found king.

'Faith' is, for Paul, partly about our personal trust in God and the gospel; partly about our belief in the central gospel events (the death and **resurrection** of Jesus); and partly about our continuing faithfulness to the God who has revealed himself in these events and in the gospel message about them. And it is this central, if complex, quality that is likely to be under attack, particularly of course when the church is being persecuted. 'Can you really', whisper the voices inside your head, and perhaps the voices of friends or family, 'can you really trust a God who lets such things happen? Can you really believe the strange events about Jesus? Can you really go on with your devotion and loyalty to this God, this king, when it would be so much easier to bow the knee once more to the pagan idols, and to Caesar himself?'

Paul knows that they will hear these voices. He knows that behind such whispers there lurks 'the tempter', testing them and perhaps undermining their faith. He doesn't know how they will respond. He can't bear the thought that all his work in Thessalonica might be destroyed, that he would go back one day and find the church disappeared, with its members looking back on their brief encounter with him like people emerging from a strange, powerful, but short-lived infatuation. So he sends Timothy not just to find out how they are, but to give them strength by his presence and teaching. The sufferings they are enduring are not a strange thing that mean God is no longer reliable. They are precisely what one ought to expect if one is following Jesus.

This is hard teaching, of course, both for those who are enduring persecution, as many Christians in the world still are, and for those who are not, or not so obviously. But the fact that suffering is inevitable for those who try to be loyal to Jesus was built in to the gospel from the beginning, and versions of Christianity which manage to avoid it are thereby called into question. Do we or do we not follow a crucified Lord?

1 THESSALONIANS 3.6–10

Timothy's Report

6But now Timothy has returned to us from you. He has brought us the good news of your faith – and your love; he has told us that you always have good memories of us, and that you are longing to see us, just as we are to see you. 7So, my dear family, we are comforted about you, in all our difficulties and troubles, because of your faithfulness. 8Now, you see, we are really alive, if you are standing firmly in the Lord. 9For what thanks can we give back to God about you, for all the joy which we celebrate because of you in the presence of our God, 10praying with even more fervour than you can imagine, night and day, that we may see your face, and may put into proper order anything that is lacking in your faith?

Learning to read Paul is a bit like learning to enjoy great music. It's quite easy to whistle a tune that you've heard on the radio or sung in church. The tune probably only lasts for ten seconds or so, and you can recognize and remember it. But many great composers have not only written wonderful tunes; they have woven them into much longer compositions – symphonies, concertos, operas and so on – in an astonishing variety of patterns, so that the pattern itself becomes a sort of new, larger tune, harder to whistle as you walk down the street, but even more satisfying when you can listen to it, understand what's going on, and hear the large tunes and the small ones together and see how it all fits.

At the end of this paragraph, and then in the closing three verses of chapter 3, we realize, if we are listening closely, that throughout this long description of his relationship with the Thessalonians – his first arrival, his work among them, his anxiety after his departure, his sending of Timothy – Paul is not simply reminiscing. He is thanking God for them and praying to God for them. What we have been listening to is framed within the explicit thanksgiving at the start of chapter 1 and the thanksgiving and prayer into which Paul now moves. Perhaps this itself serves as a good model for missionary and pastoral work: when praying, to think back in the presence of God through one's entire relationship with the church, mulling it over, learning to see God's strange design in what has gone on, earnestly asking God to complete and bring to perfection the work he has begun.

Once we try to imagine a world without electronic communications, and without a reliable or speedy public postal service, we can imagine the huge relief Paul felt when Timothy came back from Thessalonica with excellent news about the church. Paul, meanwhile, had most likely left Athens and was now in Corinth; he had had much to cope with in both places, as he indicates near the start of his first surviving letter to Corinth itself (1 Corinthians 2.3). On top of it all was his anxiety about the churches further away in northern Greece. Timothy's report was indeed 'good news'; the word Paul uses is the same as the word for preaching the **gospel**. It must have felt as though he'd heard the gospel all over again when news reached him of God's power and love at work, in his absence, in Thessalonica.

In particular – and this will remind us of his opening remarks in 1.3 – he is delighted to hear not only about their faithfulness, but also about their love. This love (Paul here focuses on their love for him and his colleagues, but in the next chapter he will speak also about their love for one another) was truly one of the astonishing things in the early church. Imagine, within that world, a new community where people from different social, cultural and racial backgrounds treated each other with the love appropriate within a family! This was a sign, which Paul regularly celebrated, of God's dramatic work, starting something quite new, the like of which the world had not seen before. It was evidence that in Jesus, and by his **spirit**, the living God was indeed at work. No wonder Paul, in the midst of his own difficulties and the opposition that met him in Athens and Corinth, found himself buoyed up. 'Now we are truly alive!' he says, 'if you are standing fast in the Lord' – in other words, if your life of allegiance to the Lord, and membership in his family, is really going so well. Paul senses the life of God at work afresh in him, too, as a result of hearing this 'good news'.

So he returns to the central task and joy of his life: thanking and praising God for all that he has done and is doing, and praying for a closer bond yet with the churches he has founded. Paul's life, with all its day-and-night hard physical work (2.9), was also a matter of day-and-night prayer, realizing that he could never thank God enough for what he had done and was doing, and that through prayer God would do yet greater things.

In particular, Paul knows that there is yet more for the Thessalonians to face. More trials to their **faith** are on the way. They have met the first tests; will they meet the next ones? And so he prays not only that he will be able to see them again soon, but also that, when he does, he will be able to supply anything that may be needed to make their faith (in all senses: belief, trust, faithfulness and loyalty) grow yet stronger and stand firm for the future. He doesn't say there is anything wrong with their faith at present; he only implies that faith needs to grow with every day, with each new trial or test, and that maybe his own further teaching and encouragement will be needed to help that to happen.

The word he uses to describe his prayer is a rare one, meaning more or less 'even more exceedingly than you can imagine'. Could you describe your own prayer in that way? If you are a pastor or teacher, is that how you pray for those in your care? If not, what is it about your vision of God and the gospel that is allowing you to be satisfied with less?

1 THESSALONIANS 3.11–13

Paul's Words of Blessing

[11]Now may God himself, our father, and our Lord Jesus, steer us on our way to you. [12]And may the Lord make your love for one another, and for everybody, abound and overflow, just as ours does for you. [13]That way, your hearts will be strengthened and kept blameless in holiness before God our father when our Lord Jesus is present again with all his holy ones. Amen.

Prayer and music have always gone together in the Christian church, and another musical illustration may help us find ways of making Paul's prayers our own. When children begin to learn a musical instrument, or to sing, the teacher often plays alongside them. The children hear the music from the teacher mixed in with the sounds they are making, and this encourages them to work together, to copy the teacher and make the same noises. It will take time, of course; and often the noise of youthful music-making is some way from being pleasant to listen to on its own, or even with a teacher. But as children grow in confidence, they move step by step towards the day when they can play without the teacher there, and may even in due course become teachers themselves.

So it is with prayer. By ourselves we have an instinct to pray, just as many people have an instinct for making music. But if this is left untaught and unguided, it will often produce the equivalent, in prayer, of the adult whose music-making consists of picking out a few tunes on a piano with one finger, or of singing only the easiest of tunes. Better than nothing, of course; but how much better to be able to make the music you are really capable of! And how much better, in learning to pray, to grow beyond a few short childish sentences, or the emergency prayers that we find ourselves praying when we are in trouble, and to become real grown-up praying people, able in due course to help others too.

So what can we learn from this short but deep prayer of Paul's?

First, we learn that prayer is grounded in the life and work of God himself – the God we come to know, through Jesus, as father. Twice in this short prayer Paul draws together God the father and Jesus the Lord, and there are signs throughout his writing that this was one of his regular ways of thinking about and addressing God and Jesus together. This isn't simply a matter of getting the labels right for the God we are talking to. Prayer that is grounded in the character of God, as revealed in Jesus, is prayer that is learning to depend on the goodness, the generosity, the sovereign love, of this God as they are unveiled in Jesus' saving death and triumphant **resurrection**. Prayer, at its very heart, is an exploration into the heart and character of God himself, not so much for the sake of enjoying being there (though that will come, too) but for the sake of bringing before this God the church and the world that need his healing love.

Prayer that acknowledges this God, this Lord, is prayer that will grow in confidence. If God is truly God, and if Jesus is truly the Lord of the world, we don't pray like people who are hoping that this God, this Lord, may somehow be able to pull off a clever move despite the power of other gods and lords. We pray with confidence to the one who is supreme over all, and who can do far more than all we can ask or think (Ephesians 3.20).

Prayer of this sort is also prayer with a future reference. It knows that this God intends one day to bring **heaven** and earth together in a new way, with the personal presence of Jesus as the central feature of this new world. Jesus will come again, 'and all his holy ones with him'; this is a quotation from one of the great Old Testament statements of hope (Zechariah 14.5), which Paul takes as referring to the final appearing of Jesus and all those who belong to him. The Lord's Prayer, too, has a strong future dimension: when we pray for daily bread, for forgiveness, and for deliverance from evil, we do so having already prayed for God's **kingdom** to come. Thus Paul's prayer for his own plans to visit northern Greece again, for the church to become a place where love is so plentiful that it seems to be overflowing from every corner, and for the Christians to be established with blameless and holy hearts – these are not simply miscellaneous requests. They focus on things that will make full sense at the great coming day of the presence of God and of Jesus.

Focused on God; looking eagerly towards God's future; and praying, in effect, for the work of God's **spirit** in the present. Some have wondered where the spirit is when Paul mentions God and Jesus so closely and frequently together. The proper answer is that the spirit is the one who is inspiring the prayer itself in Paul and his friends, and who is the hidden agency at work in the church to produce the results God and his people long to see. It is the spirit who enables Christians to love one another, and those outside the church, with a love whose supply never dries up no matter what demands are made on it. It is the spirit who settles the hearts of God's people to strive after holiness, to live without blame before God, and to become established and strengthened in that way of life. It is the spirit who is at work in the present to prepare all God's people to be what he wants them to be when he appears again.

This brief but powerful prayer thus draws together all that Paul has said so far in the letter, and prepares the ground for the particular practical and theological points he wants to make in what is to come. What will happen if we make Paul's prayer a pattern for our own? Can we listen for the tunes he's playing, and begin to play them alongside him?

1 THESSALONIANS 4.1–8

Instructions on Holy Living

¹What remains, my dear family, is for me to ask you, and indeed to urge you in the Lord Jesus, that you should continue more and more to behave in the manner that you received from us as the appropriate way of behaving and of pleasing God. ²You know, of course, what instructions we gave you through the Lord Jesus. ³This is God's will, you see: he wants you to be holy, to keep well away from fornication. ⁴Each of you should know how to control your own body in holiness and honour, ⁵not in the madness of lust like Gentiles who don't know God. ⁶Nobody should break this rule, or cheat a fellow-Christian in this area; the Lord is the avenger in all such matters, just as we told you before and testified most solemnly. ⁷For God did not call us to a dirty life, but in holiness. Anyone who rejects this, then, is not rejecting a human command, but the God who gives his holy spirit to you.

St Francis, famously, referred to his own body as 'brother donkey'. It was a beloved part of himself, and yet it often seemed to have a mind of its own. It needed taming, bringing into obedience, as one would teach a large and headstrong animal to do as it was told. The perfect partnership of rider and mount, in which the animal knows what the rider wants and takes delight and pride in doing it, is not a bad image of the perfect partnership between the indwelling of the **holy**

spirit in someone's life and the body's recognition of, and obedience to, the spirit's desires and promptings.

If we needed any reminding that human nature hasn't changed much in the last 2,000 years, the subject-matter of this chapter should provide it. When Paul wants to talk about the practical things facing the young church, the first three that come to mind are: sex, money and death. You can't get much more basic than that. His teaching, though sometimes put in a surprising way, is clear and foundational, and all depends once more on three things: the commands of the Lord, the presence of God, and the power of the spirit. Genuine Christian living always emerges in a trinitarian shape.

Paul had given the church basic rules to guide their everyday living. He handed these on to them as part of the foundational guidelines common to all the churches. He knew that the Thessalonian Christians were making every effort to keep to these, and he wanted to encourage and help them to do so more and more thoroughly.

That way, they would actually 'please God'. Sometimes people whose parents or teachers have seemed impossible to please when they were growing up think of God as someone who will barely be satisfied with our best efforts. Others are so anxious about our not being justified 'by works' that they imply that we can never do anything at all that pleases God, even as Christians indwelt by the spirit. Perhaps these two problems sometimes go together. In any case, the conclusion is false. God longs for us to become the sort of humans who will truly reflect his image. When he sees this happen, he is delighted, like a wise and generous parent with a child who starts to be a cheerful and responsible member of the family.

The word which sums up God's desire for his children, not least in the use of their bodies, is 'holiness'. People have often regarded holiness as a negative quality – the absence of moral fault – but it is actually a positive thing, the shining reflection that appears in human character when we learn in practice what it means to be in God's image. The word 'holiness' occurs three times in this passage (verses 3, 4, 7), and it draws its strength, for Paul, from the circle of ideas that belonged with the **Temple** in Jerusalem. If you went there to be in God's presence, holiness was mandatory. Special purification rituals were prescribed. It was vital that you come before the living God, the ultimately and utterly holy one, in a state of complete purity. Paul believes, of course, that Jesus' death has purified his people from all their sins. God's spirit now dwells in them: as individuals, and all together, they become the new Temple for God to live in (1 Corinthians 3.17; 6.19). They must therefore be as holy in all the details of their lives as if they were constantly in the Temple in Jerusalem.

One central concern of holiness is the area of sexuality. Our modern world has turned sexual desire, preference and practice into a moral free-for-all, where the only rule is that people must be allowed to express whatever desires happen to arise, or be aroused, within them. For Paul, as for all Jewish and early Christian teachers of moral behaviour, that is like saying that you must allow the horse or donkey, unbroken and untamed, to rush and leap about in all directions, endangering rider and onlookers alike, and doing no useful work. Sexuality is a good gift of the wise creator, but like all good gifts is given for a purpose; only in a world where the only purpose was self-gratification could anyone suppose that hard work was not going to be necessary to tame and train powerful desires such as the sexual one.

Just such a world, of course – the world of unbridled self-gratification – was what the Thessalonians found on their doorsteps, the world to which until recently they had themselves belonged. Pagan temples regularly doubled as brothels, and sexual practices of all sorts were at least tolerated if not actively encouraged within the society as a whole. The new way of life was therefore a huge challenge for the young Christians, though we may suppose that they, like many converts from the murky world of selfish licentiousness, found a certain relief in the cool, clean lines of a Judaeo-Christian morality, however much the body might rebel from time to time against the strict new standards.

Paul's clear instructions, then, are these. First, no fornication (verse 3): this word includes all kinds of sexual practice outside marriage itself, and in Paul's world could refer particularly, though not exclusively, to the sacred prostitution at pagan temples. Second, self-control within marriage: the wild and untamed lust that went on the rampage looking for new partners and new pleasures was to be brought into strict submission (verses 4, 5). Third, no cheating of one another; verse 6a is probably a delicate way of referring to people effectively stealing one another's spouses. Fourth, remember that these instructions are not only from God himself, but will be backed up by the judgment of the Lord (verse 6b). Jesus himself will pronounce sentence on those who flout this basic code; and we may observe that not infrequently this judgment is anticipated in the present life by the particularly exquisite misery awaiting many who ruin healthy and deep relationships through their restless pursuit of new sexual conquests and thrills.

Sexual morality in much of the world at the start of the twenty-first century is, we might as well admit, at a low ebb. The church desperately needs to stand out from the world at this point, rather than being eager (as it sometimes appears) to go along with the world for fear of being thought negative or 'dualistic' about one of God's good gifts. (A 'dualist' is someone who thinks of the world as being composed of two quite different parts; for instance, seeing the material world as bad and the non-material world as good.) Proper sexual behaviour is not negative; again and again, it uncovers, whether in marriage or in celibacy, ways forward to a fullness of life which the debauchee or the casually immoral never discover. Appropriate sexual self-control is not dualistic, any more than taming and training a powerful and intelligent horse is demeaning for the animal. The key to it all is the knowledge of God (verse 5), the God whom the pagans do not know: the God in whose image humans were made male and female (Genesis 1.27), and who longs to see that image reflected in the holiness that the spirit is now at work to produce (verse 8).

1 THESSALONIANS 4.9–12

A Life of Love

⁹Now, about charitable concern for the whole family: I don't really need to write to you, because you yourselves have been taught by God to care for one another. ¹⁰Indeed, you are doing this for all the Christian family in the whole of Macedonia. But we urge you, my dear family, to make this an even more prominent part of your lives. ¹¹You should make it your ambition to live peacefully, to mind your own business, and to work with your own hands, just as we commanded you, ¹²so that you may behave in a way which outsiders will respect, and so that none of you may be in financial difficulties.

'I don't care too much for money,' sang the Beatles (ironically, just as they were earning millions); 'Money can't buy me love.' Now that is of course true. But 'love' is a strange word in most languages, and there are connections between love and money which surprise us. And the point of this little paragraph is that money can *express* love, and, indeed, that if the love is genuine it will find an outlet in financial generosity.

This is not always clear, because in a literal translation verse 9 simply speaks of 'love of the family' and of 'love'. Those who think of love as a set of feelings and emotions, at some distance from practical behaviour, will naturally see this simply in terms of a kindly and winsome spirit in personal relationships – which is itself, of course, greatly to be prized. But the rest of the paragraph makes it clear, as do similar passages elsewhere in the New Testament, that this 'love' is expected to issue in practical support within the Christian community, and also, as far as this may be possible, in the world outside. God's own expression of his love resulted in his total self-giving in the person and death of his son. Christian expression of the same love must have the same self-giving quality, and money is an inescapable part of that.

The first Christians, in Jerusalem, sold their property, pooled their resources, and shared the money thus gained among themselves. This was not simply, as is sometimes said, because they expected the return of Jesus and end of the world very soon. Many monastic communities, including the one that produced the **Dead Sea Scrolls**, have had similar practices without such a reason. It was more because the early Christians saw themselves as members of a *family*; and families in the ancient world, and sometimes in the modern, share all things in common, often having common ownership of a business as well as a home, and helping each other financially as need arises.

As the **gospel** spread around the Mediterranean world, there was no continuing requirement to sell property. Many Christians owned houses; that was where the little churches met. Many were in business, including people such as Lydia, whom Paul met at Philippi. But if the gospel meant what it said then the Christians should still regard themselves – as, indeed, Paul implies by the word he regularly uses to address them – as a single family. Paul's word *adelphoi*, literally 'brothers', calls up in his world the shared working and family life of a close kinship group.

The Thessalonians, to Paul's delight, were already living this life of practical love, taking care of one another financially. What's more, they seem to have extended this outreach of giving and support further afield, to the other churches of Macedonia (including, presumably, Philippi and Beroea, and quite possibly other places as well). This implies that the

Thessalonian church was both larger, and perhaps wealthier, than the others in the area. Paul wants them to build on this work and increase it. Let it overflow, he says.

The danger of such a command, of course, is that people who are capable of earning their own living might be tempted to sponge off the others, hiding under the rule of love. But if the rule of love is to work, the rule of work itself must also be clear. Christians must learn to live peaceably, that is, without the restless desire always to 'better themselves', as our phrase goes. They must mind their own business, literally and metaphorically, not always prying into what other people are doing under the guise of 'family' interest. And they must do their best to find paid employment, which Paul assumes will be manual work.

There is a twofold aim in all of this. Outsiders, looking at a new movement that made striking claims about Jesus as Lord of the world, would be interested to see what effect it had on the behaviour of the members. Financial behaviour, like sexual behaviour, is one telling indicator of the health and integrity of a movement. And, within the fellowship, those in need should be provided for. This was why the place of widows, women left without a breadwinner, so quickly became important in the early church (Acts 6.1; 1 Timothy 5.3–16). These are not side-issues, away from the real theological heart of the Christian gospel. If God has created a new family in **Christ**, and if that family is based on and characterized by nothing less than self-giving love, these things are vital. Happy the church, today, that discovers what love in practice looks and feels like.

1 THESSALONIANS 4.13–18

The Lord's Coming

¹³Now concerning those who have fallen asleep: we don't want you to remain in ignorance about them, my dear family. We don't want you to have the kind of grief that other people do,

people who do not possess a hope. ¹⁴For, you see, if we believe that Jesus died and rose, that's the way God will also bring, with Jesus, those who fell asleep through him.

¹⁵Let me explain (this is the word of the Lord I'm speaking to you!). We who are alive, who remain until the Lord is present, will not find ourselves ahead of those who fell asleep. ¹⁶The Lord himself will come down from heaven with a shouted order, with the voice of an archangel and the sound of God's trumpet. The Messiah's dead will rise first; ¹⁷then we who are alive, who are left, will be snatched up with them among the clouds, to meet the Lord in the air. And in this way we shall always be with the Lord. ¹⁸So comfort each other with these words.

How do you describe the colour blue to a blind person? If someone has never been able to see, how can you even convey the idea of colour, let alone the difference between colours?

That difficulty faces Christians whenever we talk about the new world that God intends to make one day, when Jesus himself reappears and everything is changed. Think again of colour and blindness. You might want to 'translate' your experience of colour into a different context: sound, for instance, or touch. You might describe bright red as a hard, loud colour. You might say that a gentle blue or green was soft like a cushion, or smooth and flowing like a pretty tune. You could say that yellow was prickly, like a sharp squeaky noise. You would know that all these descriptions were hopelessly inadequate, but they would at least tell the blind person something about what it was like to see colour at all, and different varieties of it.

Now put yourself in Paul's shoes as he tries to tell the Thessalonians what is going to happen at the return of the Lord. He has a practical purpose: some Christians in Thessalonica have died, and the others aren't sure what to believe about where these people are and what will happen to them. Paul is concerned that they learn appropriate Christian grief, instead of the wild and hopeless mourning that typified pagan funerals.

Paul therefore needs to describe the moment when God makes his new world. The only possible language is that of pictures. Scientists struggle even today to find the right language to describe the moment when our world came to birth; they, too, are driven to use highly colourful and metaphorical language.

Paul's starting point echoes one of the earliest Christian creeds, the short verbal formulae that summed up what the church believed: 'Jesus died and rose again' (verse 14). That little sentence, though, doesn't just give information about the past; it reveals what will happen to those who belong to Jesus. They too, if they die 'through him', that is, through being united with him, will also rise again. God will 'bring them with Jesus'. Paul is not undertaking to say exactly where the dead are, or what state they are in. It is enough to know that they are in God's care, and that, when Jesus appears again, so will they.

But his main point requires more colourful language. This is where readers have often experienced the kind of difficulty that a blind person would meet if, supposing red to be literally a hard colour, or yellow a sharp one, they would assume that all hard objects were also red, or that all needles, forks and knives were also yellow. The basic point Paul is making is that those Christians who are still alive when the great day dawns will not find themselves at an advantage over those who have died. He explains this by using one of the pictures which, when read like the hard/red or sharp/yellow misunderstandings, has misled many Christians into supposing it was a literal description of what will one day occur.

He joins together several pictures from the Old Testament, and says (verses 16–17) that the Lord will come down from **heaven**, accompanied by various dramatic signs. The dead will rise; those who are left alive (Paul says 'we', assuming here that he and his companions will be among those still living) will be caught up to meet the Lord in the air. These two verses have had a huge influence in some circles where 'the rapture' is assumed to be the main Christian hope, with people being suddenly snatched out of homes, jobs, cars and aeroplanes, leaving the rest of humankind suddenly bereft.

To read the passage like that is to make the hard/red or sharp/yellow mistake. The key is to realize what **resurrection** itself means: it doesn't mean disembodied life in some mid-air 'heaven', but the re-embodiment of God's people to live with and for God in the new, redeemed world that God will make. It would therefore be nonsense to imagine that the presently alive Christians are literally going to be snatched up into the sky, there to remain for ever. How would they then be with the others who, having died previously, will be raised and given new bodies?

When Paul talks of Jesus 'descending', he doesn't suppose that Jesus is physically above us at the moment. Heaven, where Jesus is, isn't another location within our space, but another *dimension*. The language of 'descending' is the risky metaphor – all metaphors are risky when talking of the future – that Paul here chooses. Elsewhere (e.g. Colossians 3.4) he can speak simply of Jesus 'appearing', emerging from the presently hidden world of heaven, as heaven and earth are at last united, visibly present to one another. Here he builds into the picture, confusingly for later readers, an echo of Moses going up the mountain, the trumpet-blast as he is given the **law**, and coming down again.

So when Paul talks of Christians 'being snatched up among the clouds', he is again not thinking of a literal vertical ascent. The language here is taken from Daniel 7, where 'one like a **son of man**' goes up on the clouds as he is vindicated by God after his suffering – a wonderful image not least for people like the Thessalonians who were suffering persecution and awaiting God's vindication. And their 'meeting' with the Lord doesn't mean they will then be staying in mid-air with him. They are like Roman citizens in a colony, going out to meet the emperor when he pays them a state visit, and then accompanying him back to the city itself.

Paul's purpose here is not speculation, but comfort. We, for different days, may need to change the imagery to make the point. We may find it more intelligible to speak of Christ's 'appearing' – as Paul himself does elsewhere – than his downward 'descent'. But his point is that we can be confident in God's future purposes for those Christians who have died. There will be grief, of course; but there is also hope. There will come a day when God will put all wrongs to rights, when all grief will turn to joy. Jesus will be central to that day, which will end with the unveiling of God's new world. There, those who have already died, and those who are still alive, will both alike be given renewed bodies to serve God joyfully in his new creation.

1 THESSALONIANS 5.1–11

Children of Light

[1]Now when it comes to specific times and dates, my dear family, you don't need to have anyone write to you. [2]You yourselves know very well that the day of the Lord will come like a midnight robber. [3]When people say, 'Peace and security!', then swift ruin will arrive at their doorstep, like the pains that come over a woman in labour, and they won't have a chance of escape.

[4]But as for you, my dear family – you are not in darkness. That day won't surprise you like a robber. [5]You are all children of light, children of the day! We don't belong to the night, or to darkness. [6]So, then, let's not go to sleep, like the others, but let's stay awake and remain in control of ourselves.

[7]People who sleep, you see, sleep at night. People who get drunk get drunk at night. [8]But we daytime people should be self-controlled, clothing ourselves with the breastplate of faith and love, and with the helmet of the hope of salvation; [9]because God has not placed us on the road to fury, but to gaining salvation, through our Lord Jesus the Messiah. [10]He died for us, so that whether we stay awake or go to sleep we

should live together with him. [11]So strengthen one another, and build each other up, just as you are doing.

The story is told of a minister who dreamed that he was preaching a sermon, and woke up to find it was true.

One can hardly imagine that happening to St Paul – although there is the famous story of the lad who nodded off during one of Paul's all-night teaching sessions and fell out of a window (Acts 19.7–12). But clearly Paul the traveller knew all about staying awake when one would rather be going to sleep – or perhaps we should say going *back* to sleep, because here he is talking about people who are up earlier than everybody else, staying awake to see the sunrise.

The warning to stay awake has echoes, of course, of the story of Jesus himself. He urged the **disciples** to keep watch with him in Gethsemane (Mark 14.34, 38). He warned of forthcoming events which, he said, would be like a burglar arriving when least expected (Matthew 24.43; Luke 12.39; 21.34–35). Here, in one of his earliest letters, Paul echoes what Jesus himself had said and done 20 years previously, while conscious of the need to bring the same message to hearers in a different situation.

Of course, being Paul, he isn't content with one picture (staying awake rather than going back to sleep) if four or five will do instead. The robber at night goes quite well with the command to stay awake, but actually Paul's point about staying awake belongs not so much with the danger of burglars but with the all-important difference between the old age, the age of darkness, sin and death, and the new age, the age of light, life and hope. He thus combines two quite different ideas: staying awake because of the terrible things that are about to happen (for which he supplies a further well-known biblical picture, that of the woman going suddenly into labour-pains); and staying awake because it will soon be dawn and time to put away night-time habits.

This second theme is the heart of the paragraph. For reasons that now become clear, Christians are daytime people, even though the rest of the world is still in the night. We who live in an age of travel by jet aeroplane know what happens when we cross several time zones in quick succession. Our bodies get confused; we find ourselves waking up in the middle of the night as though it were daytime. This happens, for instance, if you fly from Britain to America, or from America to Japan. Here you are, wide awake at four o'clock in the morning; your body is telling you it's already daytime.

Well, says Paul, here you are in the middle of the world's night – but the **spirit** of Jesus within you is telling you it's already daytime. You are already children of the day, children of light. God's new world has broken in upon the sad, sleepy, drunken and deadly old world. That's the meaning of the **resurrection** of Jesus, and the gift of the spirit – the life of the new world breaking in to the old. And you belong to the new world, not the old one. You are wide awake long before the full sunrise has dawned. Stay awake, then, because this is God's new reality, and it will shortly dawn upon the whole world.

Two more pictures complete the rich, if confusing, paragraph. The first is of people (night people, Paul would say) who mumble to each other in their sleep, 'Peace and security, peace and security. Everything's all right. Nothing's going to happen.' No, says Paul, everything's not all right. Sudden disaster is on the way.

Who is he talking about? Anybody who imagines that God's new world will never break in, shining the light of divine judgment and mercy into the world's dark corners. But the slogan 'peace and security' was also one of the comforting phrases that the Roman empire put out, to reassure its inhabitants around the Mediterranean that the famous 'Roman peace', established by Paul's time for more than half a century, would hold without problems. That is what Paul is really attacking. Don't trust the imperial propaganda, he says. The world will soon plunge into convulsions, bringing terror and destruction all around. Within 20 years of this letter, the warning had come true.

That is why Paul adds the last of his potentially confusing pictures. The dawn is breaking, the birth-pangs are coming upon the world, the robbers might break in at any time, and the empire itself is under threat – so you need to put on your armour! Verse 8 is a shorter version of the fuller paragraph in Ephesians 6.10–20; here he mentions only the two main defensive pieces of armour, the breastplate and helmet.

He began the letter with the trio of **faith**, hope and love (1.3), and that is how he draws it now towards its conclusion. Faith and hope are the breastplate, to ward off frontal attacks. The hope of salvation is the helmet, protecting the head itself. Underneath it all, as always in Paul, we find God's action in Jesus the **Messiah**. In verse 10 we hear again the basic Christian creed: he died for us and rose again. That is the main defence against all that the dark world can throw at the children of light.

We, like the Thessalonians, need to remind one another of this as we face a world where sudden convulsions still occur, the world into which, one day, the final dawn will break. As children of the new day, we already belong to the Messiah, as do even those who have died. (Verse 10 refers back to those who have 'fallen asleep', not in the sense of verses 6–7, where it refers to bad behaviour, but in the sense of 4.13–14, where it refers to bodily death.) Here, emerging like a clear tune out of the complex symphony of the paragraph, is Paul's main message: hold fast in faith to the **gospel** message, and you will find in it all the comfort and strength you need.

1 THESSALONIANS 5.12–22

Final Exhortations

¹²This, my dear family, is the request we make of you. Take note of those who work among you and exercise leadership over you in the Lord, ¹³those who give you instruction. Give

them the highest possible rank of love because of their work. Live at peace among yourselves.

¹⁴And, my dear family, we beg you to warn those who step out of line. Console the downcast; help the weak, be sympathetic towards everybody. ¹⁵Make sure nobody pays anyone back evil for evil. Instead, always find the way to do good to one another, and to everybody.

¹⁶Always celebrate,
¹⁷Never stop praying;
¹⁸In everything be thankful
(this is God's will for you in the Messiah Jesus);
¹⁹Don't quench the spirit,
²⁰Don't look down on prophecies,
²¹Test everything,
If something is good, hold it fast;
²²If something looks evil, keep well away.

We all learn our mother tongues without realizing that there is such a thing as grammar. By the time we are three or four, we are using nouns, verbs, prepositions and the rest to make complex and intricate sentences – just like baby birds flying at an early age without ever having studied the laws of aerodynamics.

But when you learn another language you normally have to learn at least some grammar. And, to begin with at least, most teachers have clever little ways of getting us to remember how the new language works. When I was learning French, there was one teacher who used to make up little rhymes to help us remember tricky bits of grammar. We used to sing them in class, feeling very stupid (fancy a bunch of thirteen-year-olds singing 'all pronouns come before the verb' at the tops of their voices). But when it came time for the examination, we were in good shape. Even if we hadn't got the language into our hearts by then, so that it all came naturally, we could think of the tune and the rule would come back. English spelling was another place where rhymes and songs would help. 'I before E except after C', the teacher would remind us.

Early Christianity had many little rules. Indeed, thinking of Christian behaviour as a type of language, with its own grammar, is a helpful way of understanding what teachers like Paul were trying to do. Most of us learn a kind of mother tongue of behaviour: we watch how our families and close friends behave, and assume that this is how we should act as well. If we grow up with people shouting at each other and using violence to settle quarrels, we assume that is how one should behave. If we see people cheating each other, we expect to do so ourselves. If people around us are kind and considerate, there's a good chance we will pick that up. And so on. But supposing there are other languages of behaviour, other grammars? How are we going to learn them? How will we get them into our systems?

Of course, the Christian ideal is that we should get to the point, as with a language, where we don't need to think about it at all. If you are a native speaker of, say, Swahili, and want to learn Chinese, your aim is to be able to listen and speak in Chinese without ever thinking of grammar. To the extent that you are still racking your brains about which words to use and how to form sentences, you are not yet fluent. But, as you practise, the rules will steadily become, as we say, 'second nature'. That is the aim with learning the new language of Christian behaviour.

For most of us today, as for Paul's converts, it is indeed a new language. Some people suggest that this new language will only mean anything at all when it becomes like a mother tongue – when we don't think about rules at all, but simply behave in the Christian way from the heart. Paul, they remind us, warned against **justification** by works of the **law**. Surely he can't have wanted to give us a new set of rules, which would simply replace the commands of the law?

To think like this is to miss the point. Of course the ideal is that we should have the new language of Christian behaviour written on our hearts. Paul does indeed say in various places that this is what God's **spirit** will do (e.g., Romans 2.25–29). But it doesn't happen overnight. Indeed, the way in which God's spirit does this is not simply by working secretly within the individual heart or mind, without any other intervention and without conscious effort by the person concerned – though this may and does happen in some people to some extent. Rather, God's spirit brings us to fluency in the new language of behaviour in three ways, each of which is mentioned here.

The first is through careful Christian teaching and leadership (verses 12–13). In several places Paul urges his converts to give attention, affection and appropriate financial reward (that's probably what 'love' means here; compare 4.9–12) to those who lead and teach in the church. This is, of course, the more remarkable in that the leaders and teachers themselves in Thessalonica had only been Christians a short time. Already there were some whom God had called and equipped for this work.

The second is through the mutual influence of the whole community (verses 14–15). Each Christian, and each Christian group or family, has the responsibility to look out for the needs of the others, to give comfort, warning, strengthening and example wherever necessary. It isn't enough to avoid trouble and hope for the best. One must actively go after (the relevant phrase here means 'pursue') what will be good for other Christians, and indeed for everybody.

Third, there are the equivalents of the little rules of grammar, the rhymes and memory-aids which nudge the mind in the right direction. Verses 16–22 may well be a list of these, designed for easy memorization, which Paul has put together so that his young churches will quickly learn the language of Christian behaviour. When we speak of 'learning by heart', we often mean 'by mind', with an effort of memory; but, once that effort has been made, the heart takes what is learnt into itself until it becomes second nature, like a mother tongue. That is what Paul intends with this list.

The list itself is full of joy. The early Christians knew a lot about suffering; Paul wanted them to learn how to celebrate in the midst of it. Learning to thank God for whatever he gives is sometimes difficult, but it goes with celebrating the lordship of Jesus over the world in advance of its being made public and generally recognized. And then, the simplest but most profound of basic moral rules: when you find something good, hold it fast with both hands, but keep well clear from anything that even looks as though it might be evil. Learn these lessons – as relevant today as ever they were – and you have taken the first steps to mastering the grammar of Christian behaviour.

1 THESSALONIANS 5.23–28

Final Blessings and Charge

²³Now may the God of peace make you completely holy. May your complete spirit, soul and body be kept blameless at the coming of our Lord Jesus the Messiah. ²⁴The one who calls you is faithful; he will do it.

²⁵My dear family, pray for us.

²⁶Greet the whole family with a holy kiss. ²⁷I charge you by the Lord to have this letter read to the whole family.

²⁸The grace of our Lord Jesus the Messiah be with you.

When I was ordained to the ministry of **word** and sacrament, I received many cards and letters wishing me well and assuring me of the prayers and support of family and friends. The one that made the deepest impression on me at the time – and which I can still remember clearly nearly 30 years later – quoted three words, in the original language, from verse 24 of this passage. *Pistos ho kalon*, it said: 'The one who calls you is faithful.' It was and is a wonderful phrase, undergirding both the varied ministries of the church and also the daily life of every Christian, whether child, woman or man. I thank

God for the wisdom and prayer of the saint who sent me that card.

The faithfulness of God, in fact, is one of Paul's great themes throughout his writing. He has a good deal to say about the **gospel** message concerning Jesus the **Messiah**, but the most significant thing about Jesus is that in him the living God has put into effect his faithfulness to the entire creation, to Israel, and to each member of the human race. Paul has a good deal to say about the life of the church, its unity, its suffering, and its witness before the world; but the most significant thing about the church is that it is the company of people held in existence and maintained in truth not by human will or effort but by the sheer faithfulness of God. Paul also has a lot to say about the calling of the individual Christian, to be holy in body, soul and **spirit**. But this never degenerates into a sense of the Christian simply trying hard to behave and hoping for the best. It is always backed up, as it is here, by the faithfulness of God. 'The one who calls you is faithful.'

As Paul began the letter with prayer and thanksgiving, focused on the work of the one God through Jesus the Messiah in Thessalonica, so he ends it the same way. The God of peace – a favourite title of God for Paul – is the one who will make his people holy, so that they will be blameless at the coming of Jesus. Of course, part of the means by which he will do this is the thinking, suffering and struggling of the people themselves. This is the balance that we must maintain at the heart of all Christian living. To be holy is hard work, but we believe that it is God himself, present in our hearts by the spirit, who enables us to get on and do it. Paul doesn't suggest that only a reasonable amount of holiness is required; it must be complete. Some Christians, emphasizing the boundless love of God and the doctrine of **justification** by **faith** apart from works, run the risk of underestimating the call of holiness, which Paul – who is after all the great exponent of God's love and of free justification – never did.

As with the letter as a whole, so this conclusion looks ahead to the time when Jesus will at last be once again personally present. The many New Testament pictures of what will happen on that day are, for Paul, not so important as the effect which the Christian hope should have on the believer. Knowing that there is coming a time when every knee will bow at the name of Jesus (Philippians 2.10) doesn't mean that the Christian can sit back and take it easy. He or she must learn to bow the knee to him in the present, in holiness and adoration, and to make his coming rule known in the world.

The closing verses of the letter show how deeply engrained in the early Christian mind, including that of Paul, was the basic pattern of Christian life, set out in Acts (e.g. 2.42) and echoed at several points. 'They continued', says Luke in that passage in Acts, 'in the **apostles**' teaching and fellowship, in the breaking of bread and the prayers.' Here in verses 25–27 we have the prayers; the fellowship (the 'holy kiss' or the 'kiss of peace' symbolized the rich family life and table-fellowship of God's people); and the apostle's teaching (here seen in the public reading of the letter). These were the foundations and central characteristics of the church's life, and remain so to this day. This is the way by which 'the grace of our Lord Jesus the Messiah' will be not only with the Thessalonians but also with the whole church until the Lord returns.

Looking back over the letter we can see how Paul brings together his personal involvement with the Thessalonians and his determination that they shall be grounded in faith, love and hope. The word of God which he preached from the beginning, through which God worked powerfully to create the church and build it up, is now to continue its work both through Paul's own writings and through the teaching of the local leaders. This will sustain them through the suffering they are already undergoing because of their allegiance to Jesus as king and lord. Paul has taken care to set before them the hope that, through the turbulent times that will come upon the whole world, God's **kingdom** and glory will be revealed, and that Jesus himself will at last appear again to vindicate his people and bring them ultimate comfort and salvation. In holding fast to this hope, they are to allow God's work, of making them his holy people, to have its full effect.

2 THESSALONIANS

2 THESSALONIANS 1.1–7a

Greetings and Thanksgiving

[1]Paul, Silvanus and Timothy, to the community of Thessalonians in God our father and the Lord Jesus, the Messiah: [2]grace to you and peace from God our father and the Lord Jesus, the Messiah.

[3]We owe God a constant debt of gratitude concerning you, my dear family. It is only right and proper. Your faith is growing marvellously, and the love which every single one of you has for each other is multiplying. [4]As a result, we ourselves can tell all the churches of God how proud we are of you – of your patience and loyalty in all your troubles, and in all the sufferings you are going through.

[5]All this is a clear sign of the just judgment of God, to make you thoroughly worthy of the kingdom of God, for which you are suffering – [6]since it is just, on God's part, to pay back with suffering those who inflict suffering on you, [7]and to give you, with us, respite in the midst of your sufferings.

When our four children were younger, we had to spend Christmas Day taking notes. Once the four of them began to open presents from friends and relatives, there was so much paper and string around, and so many toys, books and games all over the room, that it was difficult to remember which child had been given which presents – and, most importantly, by whom. So my wife and I would try to keep pace with the presents by scribbling down all the important details.

Because, of course, there was a job to be done next day: writing thank-you letters. Many children have come to regard this as a chore, the unpleasant side of Christmas; but it is of course part of the essence of the whole thing. Teaching God's free grace, and his gift of himself, by celebrating Christmas is one half of the story; teaching gratitude, and heartfelt thanksgiving, is the other half. Grace that doesn't produce gratitude hasn't succeeded in softening hard hearts.

139

So when Paul writes this second letter to the young church in Thessalonica he emphasizes not only that he is thanking God for them, but that it is utterly right and proper that he should do so. As a child owes a debt of gratitude to the person who has given a generous present, so Paul owes God a debt of gratitude because of all that has happened in Thessalonica. The **faith**, the love, the suffering of the new church – when Paul looked around at it all, he couldn't help thanking God all the time.

It is important for us to underline what this means about Paul's attitude to the **gospel** and to God's grace at work in it. When he announced the gospel – the message that the crucified and risen Jesus is the world's true Lord – in a town, village or city, he didn't see it simply as a set of ideas which might appeal to the rational mind of his hearers (although to be sure he believed passionately that it made sense at the deepest levels of mind and heart). Nor did he see it as offering people an emotional experience which they would simply enjoy for its own sake. He saw it as the strange vehicle or vessel of God's grace, through which the true and living God reached out to woo and win the hearts, minds, bodies and whole lives of people who up until then had not known this God.

What was the result? When people responded to the gospel with faith, believing in this God and giving their total allegiance to this Jesus; when they formed a community of love, sharing their lives with one another; and when they were prepared to suffer for their new identity – why, then Paul saw this as a gift from God himself (a Christmas present, one might almost say), a new birth for which the only proper response was heartfelt thanks to the God who had done it all from first to last. Gratitude follows grace, and prepares the heart for more grace still.

The sovereignty of God in grace, producing faith, love and patience in new believers, is matched by the sovereignty of God in judgment. Indeed, without that, grace would be ineffectual and arbitrary. God's 'righteous judgment' (verse 5) will at the end come to the rescue of those who have been loyal to God and the gospel, and have therefore been persecuted by the world that demands allegiance to its own power and its own gods. God, in his justice, will repay those who, out of allegiance to idols and their dehumanizing ways of life, have used violence against his people.

This notion of a coming judgment, in which wrongs would be righted and evil would receive its just deserts, was commonplace among Jews of Paul's day. In this Jewish thought, it was often the **Messiah** himself who would be the agent of God's judgment against the wicked. Paul, believing Jesus to be the Messiah, saw him as the one through whom this righting of old wrongs would finally be achieved (e.g. Acts 17.31; Romans 2.16).

The sufferings the Thessalonians are enduring (see 1 Thessalonians 2.14—3.5), and the patience with which they are bearing them, serve, says Paul, as a sign of this judgment of God. If they are indeed the beginning of God's **kingdom**, which will displace all human kingdoms, then it is inevitable that the world will find them a threat and a challenge, and will oppose them all it can. The world, then as now, had many 'religions', many cults, many 'gods' and 'lords' (see 1 Corinthians 8.1–6). If Paul had simply been adding another one to this list, nobody would have minded very much. But he was clearly not doing that: he was inviting his hearers to turn from all other loyalties and give full allegiance to Jesus, and to the God who has been made known in and through him. When they did, provoking a strong reaction, this was indeed a sign that the message was effective. Grace from the one true God had been at work; those who believed became a sign of it; and gratitude was the appropriate reaction, however paradoxical that might seem in the face of suffering and persecution.

That is why Paul declares that he can boast of the Thessalonians (verse 4). By the time he writes this letter he has gone on to Beroea, then to Athens, and is most likely now in

Corinth. And, in each place, part of his message has been to tell people of what happened when the gospel did its work in Thessalonica. 'Boasting' here means something rather different from 'bragging'. Paul is by no means simply telling people what a fine church-planter he is. Rather, he regards the Thessalonian church as a key bit of evidence that he is indeed an **apostle** of Jesus the Messiah. His calling and ministry are vindicated by their very existence, and now all the more by their faith, their love and their patience. If it is hard for us to think our way back to the very first generation of the gospel, and to recapture the sense of strangeness at this new plant that was blossoming in the Greek world, it is all the more important that we ask ourselves, perhaps with pencil and paper at the ready: what have we to be thankful for? What gifts have we received at God's generous hands? What are the signs of God's strange work in our own day, our own place, our own churches?

2 THESSALONIANS 1.7b–12

The Coming of Jesus

7b This will come about when the Lord Jesus is revealed from heaven with the messengers of his power, 8 in a flaming fire, meting out punishment to those who don't know God and those who don't obey the gospel of our Lord Jesus. 9 They will pay the penalty of eternal destruction from the face of the Lord and from the glory of his power, 10 when he comes to be glorified in all his holy ones, and to be marvelled at by all who believe in him, because our testimony to you was met with faith, on that day.

11 To that end we always pray for you, that our God may make you worthy of his call, and may complete every plan he has to do you good, and every work of faith in power, 12 so that the name of our Lord Jesus may be glorified in you, and you in him, according to the grace of our God and of the Lord Jesus, the Messiah.

Shortly before Christmas 1988, a Pan Am jumbo jet, en route from London to the United States, exploded in mid-air over the small Scottish town of Lockerbie. All those on board were killed, as were several on the ground where the flaming wreckage landed. At the time I am writing this, some years later, a Scottish court, meeting in Holland, has just reached a verdict of 'guilty' on the man who planted the bomb. For the relatives of the victims it has come none too soon.

They did not want vengeance. They wanted justice. Our world has become bad at distinguishing between the two. We have rightly been so appalled at actions driven by the lust for vengeance that we have found it difficult to imagine any punishment not being motivated at least in part by revenge. But, as any victim of wilful crime knows, the desire to see justice done is quite different from the desire to hurt someone because one has been hurt oneself. There is a deep sense that the world needs to be brought back into balance.

Those of us who have not been victims ought, if we are mature and wise, to share that passion for justice. Wrongs must be righted. Evil cannot for ever triumph and mock what is good. Our human systems of justice struggle to make this clear. One of the reasons the Lockerbie trial took so long to arrange was the problem of finding a neutral location, so that everyone could agree that justice was being done.

This passage is about God's justice, not his vengeance. Some translations of verse 8 use the word 'vengeance', but today this suggests quite the wrong idea. God is not a petty or arbitrary tyrant, who throws his political opponents into jail simply for being on the wrong side. God is the living and loving creator, who must either judge the world or stand accused of injustice, of letting wickedness triumph. People who have lived in societies where evil flourishes unchecked will tell you that it is a nightmare. To live in a world where that was the case for ever would be hell.

Paul's vision of the moment when God finally puts the world to rights is coloured by several biblical passages. The vivid language is full of echoes: of the **Exodus** from Egypt, where the enslaving Egyptians were warned by a succession of plagues and then overthrown in the Red Sea; of the defeat of Babylon after Israel's **exile** and enslavement there; of the great day when God comes with all his holy ones to deliver Jerusalem and defeat those who have attacked it. There are, in scripture, many moments of judgment, which are at the same time moments of deliverance for those who have clung to the God of justice and mercy and refused to be sucked into the prevailing culture of lies and wickedness.

Into this biblical picture comes the stunning news that the judgment will be in the hands of Jesus himself. This is one among many indications that Paul saw Jesus as **Messiah**, the one through whom God's justice would be brought to the nations (e.g. Isaiah 11.1–10). But of course, for Paul, Jesus is principally the crucified one, the one in whom, as well, God's love and mercy have been lavished on an undeserving world. Paul does not, in this passage, work out how all this fits together. That awaits the majestic statement in Romans. But we who struggle to understand these statements of final judgment can never forget the fuller picture.

Because in Jesus and his **gospel** the living God has been unveiled, the God in whom is all goodness, justice, mercy and truth, those who cling to wickedness, injustice, violence and lies can be described as 'those who don't know God, and who don't obey the gospel of Jesus'. Evidence of people like that was all around in Thessalonica, not only in the idols and their shrines but in the behaviour of people on the street; and, in particular, in violent opposition to the gospel and those who believed it. The small group of believers, who had been grasped by the message Paul brought them, would one day be amazed at the way in which the standards of their surrounding culture would be reversed. Idolatry and all that goes with it would be overthrown, and the God made known in Jesus would be glorified by all (verse 10).

Christians, however, cannot be complacent as they contemplate the final judgment. God's longing – and that of the **apostle** – is that the grace of God that has called them by the gospel will now do its full work in them. When that day comes they must not appear as people who began to believe but never got around to working out what it might mean in practice. They must be people who have lived up to their initial 'call'; in other words, they must allow the saving lordship of Jesus to have its way in their lives.

In describing how this works out, Paul sounds almost like the Jesus of John's gospel: 'so that the name of Jesus may be glorified in you, and you in him' is full of echoes of Jesus' great prayer in John 17. This glorifying of Jesus' name requires focused and concentrated Christian moral effort, but underneath that as well is the mystery of God's grace.

2 THESSALONIANS 2.1–12

The Lawless One

[1]Now concerning the royal presence of our Lord Jesus the Messiah, and our gathering together around him, this is our request, my dear family. [2]Please don't be suddenly blown off course in your thinking, or be unsettled, either through spiritual influence, or through a word, or through a letter supposedly from us, telling you that the day of the Lord has already arrived.

[3]Don't let anyone deceive you in any way. You see, it can't happen unless first the rebellion takes place, and the man of lawlessness, the son of destruction, is revealed. [4]He is the one who sets himself against every so-called god or cult object, and usurps their role, so that he installs himself in God's temple, and makes himself out to be a god.

[5]Don't you remember that I told you this while I was with you? [6]And now you know what is restraining him so that he

will be revealed at his proper time. [7]For the mystery of lawlessness is already at work, but the restrainer is in place – until he is taken away. [8]Then the lawless one will be revealed; and the Lord Jesus will destroy him with the breath of his mouth, and will wipe him out with the unveiling of his presence.

[9]The presence of the lawless one will be accompanied by the activity of the satan, with full power, with signs, and spurious wonders, [10]with every kind of wicked deceit over those on the way to ruin, because they did not receive the love of the truth so as to be saved. [11]For that reason God sends upon them a strong delusion, leading them to believe the lie, [12]so that judgment may come upon all who did not believe the truth but took pleasure in wickedness.

Horatio Nelson (1758–1805), England's most famous naval commander, is remembered for many things; but one of the best-known incidents in his life occurred when he was leading the siege at Copenhagen in 1801. He was informed of a signal instructing him to withdraw, which he was determined not to do. He had lost his right eye in battle seven years previously; so, placing his telescope to that eye, he declared that he really did not see the signal. He was telling the truth at one level, but was of course remaining wilfully blind to wider truth which he did not, at that moment, choose to acknowledge.

Sadly, that attitude is not confined to brilliant and headstrong naval commanders. Most us of have met people who create a web of lies around themselves, and come to believe in the false world they have invented. Sometimes, alas, such people are deeply religious, and their devotion convinces them that they cannot possibly be mistaken. The Christian **gospel**, of course, includes the Lord's Prayer, with its regular petition for forgiveness; we Christians are called to search our consciences daily for the lies which we, too, can easily create and come to believe.

Paul describes people in this self-blinded condition in verses 11–12. He is alluding once more to the story of God's rescue of Israel from Egypt: Pharaoh, king of Egypt, began by hardening his own heart against the Israelites, but in the end God himself hardened Pharaoh's heart (Exodus 4.21; 7.13; 9.12; etc.). There comes a point, it seems, when someone sinks so deeply into lies and wickedness that they pass beyond any further ability to recognize truth and goodness. At that moment (and of course only God knows when it might be) the only possibility is for them to be brought swiftly to complete error and so to judgment.

But what situation is Paul describing in the earlier part of the chapter? This passage has puzzled generations of readers.

Think of another telescope, but this time one you can see through. There are several lenses, which together create an image of the object, magnifying it so that it looks closer than it really is. The style of writing which Paul uses here is like that. He is looking, as we now realize, into the far distant future; the final judgment has not yet taken place. But he sees it through the lens of events which were unfolding in his own times.

Paul does not suppose that these events are the final ones. If 'the day of the Lord' meant 'the end of the world', the Thessalonians would not need to be informed of such an event by letter! The Old Testament prophets used 'the day of the Lord' to refer to catastrophes that befell Jerusalem within continuing history. In the same way Paul speaks of events which he sees rushing forward to meet his little churches, and through these lenses he views, at the same time, the ultimate future judgment itself. His telescoped writing style may confuse us, but for Paul there was no problem in talking in the same breath of events both near at hand and at an uncertain distance in the future.

But what were the close-up events? Shortly before Paul began his missionary journeys, there had been a major crisis in the Middle East. The Roman emperor Gaius Caligula, convinced of his own divinity, and angry with the Jews over various matters, ordered a huge statue of himself to be placed in the **Temple** in Jerusalem. Massive Jewish protests at all levels, and the anxious advice of his officers on the spot, failed to dissuade him from this provocative project. Only Gaius's sudden murder in the January of AD 41 prevented a major disaster. The Roman–Jewish war of 66–73 might easily have begun 25 years earlier.

It looks as though Paul, aware of what had nearly happened, envisaged that sooner or later some other megalomaniac would have the same idea. He speaks of a 'man of lawlessness', who elevates himself to a position of divinity, exactly as the Roman emperors were beginning to do. Paul saw this danger on the horizon, and knew that such idolatry would conflict disastrously with the true God and his Temple in Jerusalem. Had Paul lived until AD 70 he would have recognized the initial fulfilment of his words in this passage. Evil must reach its height, and then meet sudden doom. The Roman empire itself would go through unimaginable convulsions: the death of four emperors in quick succession during 68 and 69, followed by the destruction of the Jerusalem Temple, would certainly qualify, in Old Testament terms, for the title 'the day of the Lord'.

What or who, then, is 'the restrainer'? What did Paul think was holding back these awful catastrophes? We can't be sure. He may be thinking of some Jewish leader who would exercise the kind of restraining influence on the emperor that Herod Agrippa (10 BC – AD 44) had tried to exercise on his friend Gaius. Or he may be thinking of his own work, called by God to establish churches around the Mediterranean world, and trusting that God would delay the catastrophe long enough for him to complete what he had begun. Or he may have some other restraining influence, or person, in mind, that was clear to him and his readers but remains unclear to us.

What is clear, though, is Paul's firm belief that a time was coming in which God's judgment on the idolatrous world, and its blasphemous leaders, would be unveiled. Through this lens he sees, too, events further off, the final personal presence (the '**parousia**') of Jesus, who will destroy all evil and put God's just and truthful judgment into effect against those who had been taken in by lies great and small.

In particular, God will judge, during history and finally at the end of history itself, the imperial systems that put themselves in his place. There have been enough of these in our own recent past for us to see something of the way they operate, the deceits they weave, and the way in which people get caught up in the web of their lies. What Paul would have us urgently grasp is the fact that God remains sovereign over all, and will one day put all wrongs to rights, and bring all human empires under the rule and judgment of his own saving **kingdom**.

2 THESSALONIANS 2.13–17

Exhortation to Steadfastness

¹³But we always owe God a debt of gratitude for you, my family beloved by the Lord, because God chose you as the first-fruits of his work of salvation, through sanctification by the spirit and belief of the truth. ¹⁴To this he called you through our gospel, so that you might obtain the glory of our Lord Jesus the Messiah.

¹⁵So then, my dear family, stand firm, and hold on tight to the traditions which you were taught, whether through what we said or through our letter. ¹⁶And may our Lord Jesus the Messiah himself, and God our father who loved us and gave us eternal comfort and good hope by grace, comfort your hearts and strengthen you in every good work and word.

'Stand firm and hold on tight.' When did you last hear those words?

On an airport bus, perhaps, taking you from the terminal building to the plane. On a boat ferrying passengers across a busy river. On a narrow mountain ledge when a sudden storm sweeps by. At a time of movement and danger, a time when something is about to happen which might cause injury or even death. Plant both feet as solidly as you can, take hold of the safety-rope or anything else you may be able to hang on to, and brace yourself for the shock.

That is precisely the position Paul is recommending to the young church. There are troubled times on the way, and like a small boat crossing a turbulent waterway the little ship of the church is going to be tossed to and fro. When that's happening, they need to know how to stand upright and what to hold on to. Here Paul is quite clear: the safety-rope consists of 'the traditions you were taught', that is, the foundational Christian teachings which he gave them when he was with them, and then by letter.

We know from his various writings what these were. He frequently refers back to them, as for instance in 1 Corinthians chapters 11 (about the **eucharist**) and 15 (the basic **gospel** message itself). Often he says 'you will remember' or 'you know, don't you', reminding his hearers of teaching they have already received (e.g. Romans 6.3). These teachings are about three things in particular: the basic facts of the gospel; the central actions of the worshipping church, such as **baptism** and the eucharist; and the fundamental principles of Christian behaviour, particularly the mutual support he calls *agape*, 'love'. Hold on tight to these, he says, and you won't go far wrong. This is as true today as it was in the first century.

The mental and moral effort the young church must make to keep its footing and retain its grasp is surrounded on all sides by the grace and power of God. All mature Christian thinking has this two-sided nature: God is powerful and will support you, therefore you need to stand firm and hold tight. We easily suppose that, if God is in control, we can relax; or that, if we have to struggle and work hard, it means that God isn't as powerful as we had thought. That misses the point.

The way in which God's power is exercised is precisely *through* the love, the comfort and the teaching of the gospel, which don't work as it were automatically, without our conscious involvement, but which on the contrary stiffen our resolve and energize our flagging spirits. We see exactly the same balance when Paul says in 1 Corinthians 15.10 that he worked harder than all the rest – yet it was not him, but God's grace that was with him.

How does this overarching grace of God operate? In verses 13 and 14 Paul sets out a very full picture of God's grace – as full as any similar summary (compare, for instance, Romans 8.29–30; the similarity between these two passages suggests that Paul regularly said this kind of thing in his teaching). God in his love has *chosen* them to be the 'firstfruits', the pioneer project as it were, of his work of salvation. Because of this he has *called* them through the gospel, with the result that they have been 'sanctified by the **spirit**', that is, set apart for God like **priests** in the **Temple**, only now with holiness as the inner principle of their lives, not a matter of outward washings and other rituals; and, again through the gospel, they have come to **faith** – not just any religious faith, but to 'belief in the truth'. The end result of all this is that they will come to share the *glory* of Jesus **Christ** himself, the glory which he has through his **resurrection** and exaltation (compare Philippians 3.20–21). Everything that a Christian does, from belief to baptism to holiness to hope, is held within this framework of God's powerful love and grace. That is why Paul can thank God for them. All that has been accomplished in their lives is his gift, and all that will be accomplished will be to his glory.

That, too, is why Paul can finish this major part of the letter with a confident prayer and blessing. God has given us, as a free gift in Christ, his love, his eternal comfort, and his 'good hope' – 'good' both in the sense that we hope for all the good things that are ours in Christ and in the sense that this hope can be utterly relied on. These blessings, which will be ours in

151

full in the future, come forward to meet us in the present, in the form of comfort for our hearts and strength for our actions and our speech.

Considering how brief these verses are, they offer a remarkably full summary statement both of Christian theology and of Christian practice. This letter is often squeezed to one side by people who study Paul, in favour of the more obvious texts such as Romans and Galatians. But if it was the only piece of Paul that we had, we would still have quite a substantial picture of his ministry, his prayer, his thinking and his passion. Above all, we would still have his picture of God: the God of justice and grace, who in Jesus Christ has put the world to rights, and is now at work to implement that action through the spirit-filled church. So: stand firm, hold on tight, and celebrate the greatness of God!

2 THESSALONIANS 3.1–5

Requests for Prayer

[1] Finally, my dear family, pray for us, that the word of the Lord will go forward quickly and be glorified, as it has among you; [2] and that we may be rescued from evil and wicked people. Not all, you see, have faith! [3] But the Lord is faithful, and he will strengthen you and guard you from the evil one.

[4] We are confident in the Lord about you, that you are doing, and will continue to do, what we instructed you. [5] May the Lord direct your hearts towards the love of God and the patience of the Messiah.

Among all the strange dreams that visit us at night, one of the most frustrating – which happens to me quite frequently – is the dream of trying to run and discovering that it's impossible to do so. My legs feel like lead: they become hopelessly heavy, and I can hardly move them. The attempt to run becomes agonizing. Imagine the sense of freedom and release if, suddenly, the dream were to change and you could run freely and without any problem!

Having told the Thessalonians what he is praying for in relation to them, Paul asks them to pray for him. What he asks, translated literally, is that the word of the Lord will 'run and be glorified', as was the case among them. Wherever Paul went he announced the **good news**, the gospel of Jesus; this was 'the word of the Lord', the word both *from* the Lord and *about* the Lord. And Paul longed that this word might 'run', that is, that it might make its way freely into people's hearts and lives, changing them and forming them into a holy and loving people who would bring God glory in the world. But often he must have felt as though, when he preached, the word of the Lord was like a runner in a dream: trying to do its work, but being held back by strange invisible forces, hardly able to put one foot in front of the other. Certainly his experience at Athens, not long before the writing of the two letters to Thessalonica, must have seemed like that (Acts 17.16–21, 32–34).

What will break the hidden chains, and set the word of the Lord free to 'run and be glorified'? The answer is simple: prayer. It must have seemed strange to the Thessalonians, as brand new Christians, that Paul, the great **apostle**, through whom God was doing so many remarkable things, should need *their* prayers so that his work could prosper. But the God who inspires prayer by his **spirit**, and attends to it in his love, is no respecter of persons. When, at the last, each of us knows as we are known, it will become clear just how much work for God's **kingdom** has been advanced and upheld by people who remain unheard of in the wider world but who have given themselves in love and devotion to pray earnestly for the progress of the gospel.

Paul requests prayer not only for the effectiveness of his preaching of the gospel; he also asks them to pray that he may escape the clutches of wicked people. Paul has his feet on the ground. He never allows his exultation in God's love and power to blind him to the malice and sheer evil that dogs his footsteps wherever he goes. Those who have preached and lived the gospel for a while will know only too well what he means. When God's light shines into places where darkness had allowed evil to flourish undetected, it makes people nervous, then angry, then malicious. By no means everybody believes the gospel when it is preached. Those who hear it but do not believe it may well resort to plotting and violence against those who preach it. It happened to Paul much of the time, and he – like many preachers today – needed prayers for God's defence.

Once more, however, behind the preaching and praying, the work in which apostles and churches share, stands the Lord himself, who remains faithful. Here again is the paradox of Christian living: *because* the Lord is faithful and will guard us, *therefore* we pray that he will do so. This always sounds illogical to those who aren't engaged in it. Those who are will know that prayer has a power and sense which operate below and above logic. Our praying hearts, minds and lives are put at the disposal of the living Lord, who remains sovereign, but who also longs for our collaboration in his work of strengthening the church and guarding it from evil.

Paul once again turns to the church and its needs. They will, he is confident, continue to live in the way that he has taught them, incredible though it may seem that a group who a few months ago had never thought of living a Christian lifestyle should continue to do so. What they need, if they are to be able to sustain this life, is, once more, the rooting of their hearts and lives, not in any human pressure, not in any agenda from another human being, but in the love of God and the patience of the **Messiah**. Go on focusing heart and mind on Jesus himself, Paul says, and as you meditate on his patience, and his strength under suffering, something of that patience will be given to you.

As that happens, you will know God's love surrounding you and enabling you to live the next day, week and month to his glory. Christian living without prayer and meditation can indeed sometimes seem like trying to run in a dream. We all need to learn the secrets of how the word of the Lord and the love of God can be set free to run their course and bring glory to God, in our lives and in his world.

2 THESSALONIANS 3.6–13

The Dangers of Idleness

⁶Here is a command we have for you, my dear family, in the name of our Lord Jesus the Messiah. Keep away from any member of the family who is stepping out of line, and not behaving according to the tradition that you received from us.

⁷You yourselves know, after all, how you should copy us. We didn't step out of line, ⁸nor did we eat anyone's food without paying for it. We worked night and day, with labour and struggle, so as not to place a burden on any of you. ⁹It wasn't that we don't have the right; it was so that we could give you an example, for you to copy us. ¹⁰And, indeed, when we were with you, we gave you this command: those who won't work shouldn't eat!

¹¹You see, we hear that there are some among you who are stepping out of line, behaving in an unruly fashion, not being busy with real work, but just busybodies. ¹²To people like that we give this commandment and exhortation in the Lord Jesus the Messiah: do your own work in peace, and eat your own bread. ¹³As for you, my dear family, don't get tired of doing what is right!

The dancers swept on to the stage in perfect formation. It was breathtaking. Even I, who know almost nothing about ballet, found the whole performance enthralling. And part of the beauty of a well-performed ballet is the way in which the individual and the group work perfectly together. Every individual must dance his or her particular part exactly right in order that the whole ensemble can stay in exactly the right line, without a single toe or heel out of place. It takes years of training to dance like that, of course, and hours of practice for each particular sequence. But the effect is worth the work.

Three times in this passage Paul uses a word which could have been applied to a dancer who lost concentration for a moment, and allowed a foot, or an elbow, to move just a little out of line. Watch out for those who step out of line, he says (verse 6). We didn't step out of line when we were with you (verse 7); but I hear that some are stepping out of line (verse 11). The dance is being damaged. The flow of the drama is interrupted. The spectators will see that something is amiss. Every individual must take care to stay exactly in line so that the whole ensemble may have its desired effect.

What is the particular problem? It is a problem that only appears in a community that is seriously attempting to live *as a family*, in mutual financial support. As in 1 Thessalonians 4.9–12, Paul is firmly committed to the church putting into practice a kind of love, *agape*, which is not simply a matter of feeling warmly towards one another (though that, one hopes, will be the case), nor yet a matter of treating one another kindly and with sincere friendship (though that, too, is vital), but rather of actual financial support. Paul did not require, as the early Jerusalem church had done, that converts should make over their property into a common purse. Most still owned houses, shops, and the various personal belongings typical of the time. But he did require that all the members of a church should be committed to sharing with one another as each had need, as would be the case in a Mediterranean family of the period. That is one of the meanings behind his regular way of speaking to his churches as 'family', 'brothers and sisters'.

The problem with this is that it is all too easy for some in such a community to slacken their own work and to rely on the efforts of others. This, he says, is stepping out of line. When Paul had been with them, even though as an **apostle** he had the right to have them pay for his upkeep (and he was keen that church leaders should be financially supported, as we see in 1 Corinthians 9 and 1 Thessalonians 5.12–13), he refused to make use of this right, in order to set them an example. Each member should work at whatever occupation they could, so as to contribute to the welfare of all; and all should care for each. Love must not be taken for a ride, must not be taken for granted. Love doesn't mean trading on the goodwill of others – or allowing others to trade on yours. To receive love, as well as to give it, one must not step out of line.

It appears that some in Thessalonica had been out of line in just this way. 'Busybodies', Paul calls them, going around visiting people, showing up here and there, but never actually settling to a job of work, relying instead on the goodwill of other Christians. Some have suggested that this behaviour was caused by the idea that the world was very soon going to come to an end, but this is probably not the main reason. The main reason was Paul's teaching that the church was indeed a family, and that its members should therefore take care of one another. Just as in any household it is sometimes tempting for one member to sneak out of regular domestic duties, and rely on the others to be 'nice' and 'not make a fuss' – trading on their 'love' to get a free ride – so it can be in the church. But that isn't the way that the dance of God's love sweeps on to the stage and brings gasps of delight from the onlookers.

Paul's remedy is swift and effective. Such people should be shunned. In theatrical terms, they should be sent back to the wings, or back to dancing school, until they can learn what it means to keep in line. Most modern Western churches hate the idea of discipline; it seems so 'unloving'. Of course there is such a thing as harsh or self-serving discipline. But if there is a genuine problem the sooner it is dealt with the better. Otherwise one is actually being unloving to everybody else.

And in this case Paul's rule is striking: no work, no food! Of course there are always some who, through age or illness, simply can't work. They must be supported. But if someone simply doesn't want to work – well, they should be made to see the instant connection between their idleness and the community budget. They aren't putting anything in; they shouldn't get anything out. (We note, once more, that this assumes common distribution of food, perhaps even regular eating of main meals together.)

The final word is one of Paul's regular commands. Don't get tired of doing what is right. It is very easy to become tired when you see, all around, people who are living in a different way, including some of your own number stepping out of line. But the dance must go on, and even though you may be tired you mustn't lose concentration. Listen to the music of love that sweeps through the hall. Watch your fellow Christians carefully as together you sweep out onto the stage of the world. And don't step out of line.

2 THESSALONIANS 3.14–18

Final Remarks

[14]If anyone doesn't obey our word in this letter, take note of them. Don't have any dealings with such a person, so that they may be ashamed. [15]Don't consider a person like this an enemy: rebuke them as a member of the family. [16]Now may the Lord of peace give you peace always in every way. The Lord be with you all.

[17]I, Paul, am sending you this greeting in my own hand. This is the sign in each letter of mine; this is how I write. [18]The grace of our Lord Jesus the Messiah be with you all.

Every parent knows that there are times when a child has to be punished. No parent worthy of the name will want to do so in anger and bitterness. Every true father or mother faces the difficult task of communicating to a child the fact that, precisely because they love them so much, they must now impose some kind of sanction. The child will sometimes need to learn the hard way what, we assume, the parents had tried to teach by word and example. In such a case, it is failure to discipline, not discipline itself, that would be the sign of a lack of love.

Such discipline will vary from case to case, culture to culture, and family to family. Paul here envisages that, in the tight-knit world of small-town family life known to most of his church members, there were appropriate styles of discipline within a family, ways of making it known to a child or a sibling that a particular kind of behaviour was unacceptable. But nobody would normally suppose that such discipline meant the person concerned was being kicked out of the family for good. On the contrary, it was because they still belonged to the family that discipline was necessary.

That is the background against which he commands that people who will not pay attention to the letter he has just written must be regarded as family members in need of discipline. The simplest form of such discipline is simply to exclude them from the common life. In a family this might mean sending the offending member to his or her room, or making them eat at a separate table.

Most Western Christians in mainline churches are almost completely unfamiliar with this sort of discipline – though I have known cases where flagrant immorality or financial dishonesty required a bishop or church leader to forbid the offender to attend the **eucharist** until they demonstrated their **repentance**. Much contemporary culture has reacted so strongly against the abuse of power, and then against the *exercise* of power or discipline in any sphere, that the mere suggestion of it conjures up images of people being burnt at the stake, or of the horrors of the Inquisition. We now have so embraced the idea of everyone being free to follow their own way that we recoil from the suggestion of 'sending someone to Coventry' like this. That is a healthy reaction, but it mustn't become an overreaction.

The result, of course, is that we do the same thing by other means. If we dislike someone, or disapprove of what they've done, we may well simply stop going to the church where they worship, or stop frequenting places where we will meet them. Most modern Christians have that option; the Thessalonians didn't. There were only a few of them, and there were no other churches. They had to deal with the problem head on, just as in a family or a small village. Unless the whole family remained loyal to the **gospel**, pretty soon they would cease to exist altogether.

The difficult notion of discipline rests, of course, on another notion many today find difficult: apostolic authority. We are far more inclined, in leadership roles, to suggest to people that they might perhaps like to do this or that, rather than to tell them that this is how things *must* be done. Again, of course, sooner or later someone has to make decisions, from the ordering of worship to the moral standards that will hold the community's life together. Unless there is a clear authority structure something else will take its place, quite possibly the force of certain personalities or the loudness of certain voices. The value of a clear system of authority (though it, too, is of course always open to abuse) is that it avoids allowing things to degenerate into bullying by the powerful or sniping by the petulant. Paul believed – he staked his life on it – that God had given him this authority, not to lord it over his churches, but to keep them in line, like young saplings being tied to a rod until they had the strength to stand firm on their own. Today's churches need to know how authority should work in their different situations, not least as we face a world where all authority is suspect and many in the churches appear to prefer anarchy.

Like many modern writers, Paul employed secretaries who would take down his dictation. He would then, at the end, take the pen and write the final greeting. The Thessalonians may well have received letters that purported to come from him but didn't (see e.g. 2.2); some have even thought that this letter itself was written by someone else, though many scholars rightly reject this as over-clever and unnecessary. In any case, Paul is determined that they shall know that this one is indeed from him. Here is his signature, and they should recognize his writing.

As always, underneath everything he says, does and writes, the bottom line is grace. 'The grace of our Lord Jesus Christ.'

Think carefully about that little phrase, which comes so easily to a Christian's lips. Ponder the fact that twenty-five years or so before this letter was written nobody outside a small town in northern Palestine had even heard the name of Jesus of Nazareth, let alone used the words 'Lord' and '**Messiah**' in connection with him. Now, people in an important city in Macedonia were not only hailing him with these royal titles; they were looking to him to supply 'grace' – the powerful love of the one true God, flooding and transforming their lives and their world.

But now, think of this: this same Jesus, this king, this Lord, is ready to pour that same grace on you, your community, your world. All he requires is that you should respond to his love and faithfulness with an answering love and faithfulness of your own. And you will find, like the Thessalonians, the way to a life of gratitude and hope.

GLOSSARY

apostle, disciple

'Apostle' means 'one who is sent'. It could be used of an ambassador or official delegate. In the New Testament it is sometimes used specifically of Jesus' inner circle of twelve; but Paul sees not only himself but several others outside the Twelve as 'apostles', the criterion being whether the person had personally seen the risen Jesus. Jesus' own choice of twelve close associates symbolized his plan to renew God's people, Israel (who traditionally thought of themselves as having twelve tribes); after the death of Judas Iscariot (Matthew 27.5; Acts 1.18) Matthias was chosen by lot to take his place, preserving the symbolic meaning. During Jesus' lifetime they, and many other followers, were seen as his 'disciples', which means 'pupils' or 'apprentices'.

baptism

Literally, 'plunging' people into water. From within a wider Jewish tradition of ritual washings and bathings, **John the Baptist** undertook a vocation of baptizing people in the Jordan, not as one ritual among others but as a unique moment of **repentance**, preparing them for the coming of the **kingdom of God**. Jesus himself was baptized by John, identifying himself with this renewal movement and developing it in his own way. His followers in turn baptized others. After his **resurrection**, and the sending of the **Holy Spirit**, baptism became the normal sign and means of entry into the community of Jesus' people. As early as Paul it was aligned both with the Exodus from Egypt (1 Corinthians 10.2) and with Jesus' death and resurrection (Romans 6.2–11).

Christ, *see* **Messiah**

circumcision, circumcised

The cutting off of the foreskin. Male circumcision was a major mark of identity for Jews, following its initial commandment to Abraham (Genesis 17), reinforced by Joshua (Joshua 5.2–9). Other peoples, e.g. the Egyptians, also circumcised male children. A line of thought from Deuteronomy (e.g. 30.6), through Jeremiah (e.g. 31.33), to the **Dead Sea Scrolls** and the New Testament (e.g. Romans 2.29) speaks of 'circumcision of the heart' as God's real desire, by which one may become inwardly what the male Jew is outwardly, that is, marked out as part of God's people. At periods of Jewish assimilation into the surrounding culture, some Jews tried to remove the marks of circumcision (e.g. 1 Maccabees 1.11–15).

covenant

At the heart of Jewish belief is the conviction that the one God, YHWH, who had made the whole world, had called Abraham and his family to belong to him in a special way. The promises God made to Abraham and his family, and the requirements that were laid on them as a result, came to be seen in terms either of the agreement that a king would make with a subject people, or of the marriage bond between husband and wife. One regular way of describing this relationship was 'covenant', which can thus include both promise and law. The covenant was renewed at Mount Sinai with the giving of the **Torah**; in Deuteronomy before the entry to the Promised Land; and, in a more focused way, with David (e.g. Psalm 89). Jeremiah 31 promised that after the punishment of **exile** God would make a 'new covenant' with his people, forgiving them and binding them to him more intimately. Jesus believed that this was coming true through his **kingdom**-proclamation and his death and **resurrection**. The early Christians developed these ideas in various ways, believing that in Jesus the promises had at last been fulfilled.

Dead Sea Scrolls

A collection of texts, some in remarkably good repair, some extremely fragmentary, found in the late 1940s around Qumran (near the north-east corner of the Dead Sea), and virtually all now edited, translated and in the public domain. They formed all or part of the library of a strict monastic group, most likely Essenes, founded in the mid-second century BC and lasting until the Jewish–Roman war of AD 66–70. The scrolls include the earliest existing manuscripts of the Hebrew and Aramaic scriptures, and several other important documents of community regulations, scriptural exegesis, hymns, wisdom writings, and other literature. They shed a flood of light on one small segment within the Judaism of Jesus' day, helping us to understand how some Jews at least were thinking, praying and reading scripture. Despite attempts to prove the contrary, they make no reference to **John the Baptist**, Jesus, Paul, James or early Christianity in general.

disciple, *see* **apostle**

eternal life, *see* **present age**

eucharist

The meal in which the earliest Christians, and Christians ever since, obeyed Jesus' command to 'do this in remembrance of him' at the Last Supper (Luke 22.19; 1 Corinthians 11.23–26). The word 'eucharist' itself comes from the Greek for 'thanksgiving'; it means, basically, 'the thank-you meal', and looks back to the many times when Jesus took bread, gave thanks for it, broke it, and gave it to people (e.g. Luke 24.30; John 6.11). Other early phrases for the same meal are 'the Lord's supper' (1 Corinthians 11.20) and 'the breaking of bread' (Acts 2.42). Later it came to be called 'the Mass' (from the Latin word at the end of the service, meaning 'sent out') and 'Holy Communion' (Paul speaks of 'sharing' or 'communion' in the body and blood of Christ). Later theological controversies about the precise meaning of the various actions and elements of the meal should not obscure its centrality in earliest Christian living and its continuing vital importance today.

exile

Deuteronomy (29—30) warned that if Israel disobeyed YHWH, he would send his people into exile, but that if they then repented he would bring them back. When the Babylonians sacked Jerusalem and took the people into exile, prophets such as Jeremiah interpreted this as the fulfilment of this prophecy, and made further promises about how long exile would last (70 years, according to Jeremiah 25.12; 29.10). Sure enough, exiles began to return in the late sixth century BC (Ezra 1.1). However, the post-exilic period was largely a disappointment, since the people were still enslaved to foreigners (Nehemiah 9.36); and at the height of persecution by the Syrians Daniel 9.2, 24 spoke of the 'real' exile lasting not for 70 years but for 70 *weeks* of years, i.e. 490 years. Longing for the real 'return from exile', when the prophecies of Isaiah, Jeremiah, etc. would be fulfilled, and redemption from pagan oppression accomplished, continued to characterize many Jewish movements, and was a major theme in Jesus' proclamation and his summons to **repentance**.

Exodus

The Exodus from Egypt took place, according to the book of that name, under the leadership of Moses, after long years in which the Israelites had been enslaved there. (According to Genesis 15.13f., this was itself part of God's covenanted promise to Abraham.) It demonstrated, to them and to Pharaoh, King of Egypt, that Israel was God's special child (Exodus 4.22). They then wandered through the Sinai wilderness for 40 years, led by God in a pillar of cloud and fire; early on in this time they were given the **Torah** on Mount Sinai itself. Finally, after the death of Moses and under the leadership of Joshua, they crossed the Jordan and entered, and eventually conquered, the Promised Land of Canaan. This event, commemorated annually in Passover and other Jewish festivals, gave the Israelites not only a powerful memory of what had made them a people, but also a particular shape and content to their faith in YHWH as not only creator but also redeemer; and in subsequent enslavements, particularly the **exile**, they looked for a further redemption which would be, in effect, a new Exodus. Probably no other past event so dominated the imagination of first-century Jews; among them the early Christians, following the lead of Jesus himself, continually referred back to the Exodus to give meaning and shape to their own critical events, most particularly Jesus' death and **resurrection**.

faith

Faith in the New Testament covers a wide area of human trust and trustworthiness, merging into love at one end of the scale and loyalty at the other. Within Jewish and Christian thinking faith in God also includes *belief*, accepting certain things as true about God, and what he has done in the world (e.g. bringing Israel out of Egypt; raising Jesus from the dead). For Jesus, 'faith' often seems to mean 'recognizing that God is decisively at work to bring the **kingdom** through Jesus'. For Paul, 'faith' is both the specific belief that Jesus is Lord and that God raised him from the dead (Romans 10.9) and the response of grateful human love to sovereign divine love (Galatians 2.20). This faith is, for Paul, the solitary badge of membership in God's people in Christ, marking them out in a way that **Torah**, and the works it prescribes, can never do.

Gentiles

The Jews divided the world into Jews and non-Jews. The Hebrew word for non-Jews, *goyim*, carries overtones both of family identity (i.e. not of Jewish ancestry) and of worship (i.e. of idols, not of the one true God YHWH). Though many Jews established good relations with Gentiles, not least in the Jewish Diaspora (the dispersion of Jews away from Palestine), officially there were taboos against contact such as intermarriage. In the New Testament the Greek word *ethne*, 'nations', carries the same meanings as *goyim*. Part of Paul's overmastering agenda was to insist that Gentiles who believed in Jesus had full rights in the Christian community alongside believing Jews, without having to become **circumcised**.

good news, gospel, message, word

The idea of 'good news', for which an older English word is 'gospel', had two principal meanings for first-century Jews. First, with roots in Isaiah, it meant the news of YHWH's long-awaited victory over evil and rescue of his people. Second, it was used in the Roman world for the accession, or birthday, of the emperor. Since for Jesus and Paul the announcement of God's inbreaking **kingdom** was both the fulfilment of prophecy and a challenge to the world's present rulers, 'gospel' became an important shorthand for both the message of Jesus himself and the apostolic message about him. Paul saw this message as itself the vehicle of God's saving power (Romans 1.16; 1 Thessalonians 2.13).

The four canonical 'gospels' tell the story of Jesus in such a way as to bring out both these aspects (unlike some other so-called 'gospels' circulated in the second and subsequent centuries, which tended both to cut off the scriptural and Jewish roots of Jesus' achievement and to inculcate a private spirituality rather than confrontation with the world's rulers). Since in Isaiah this creative, life-giving good news was seen as God's own powerful word (40.8; 55.11), the early Christians could use 'word' or 'message' as another shorthand for the basic Christian proclamation.

gospel, *see* **good news**

heaven

Heaven is God's dimension of the created order (Genesis 1.1; Psalm 115.16; Matthew 6.9), whereas 'earth' is the world of space, time and matter that we know. 'Heaven' thus sometimes stands, reverentially, for 'God' (as in Matthew's regular '**kingdom** of heaven'). Normally hidden from human sight, heaven is occasionally revealed or unveiled so that people can see God's dimension of ordinary life (e.g. 2 Kings 6.17; Revelation 1, 4—5). Heaven in the New Testament is thus not usually seen as the place where God's people go after death; at the end, the New Jerusalem descends *from* heaven *to* earth, joining the two dimensions for ever. 'Entering the kingdom of heaven' does not mean 'going to heaven after death', but belonging in the present to the people who steer their earthly course by the standards and purposes of heaven (cf. the Lord's Prayer: 'on earth as in heaven', Matthew 6. 10), and who are assured of membership in the age to come.

high priest, *see* **priest**

holy spirit

In Genesis 1.2, the spirit is God's presence and power *within* creation, without God being identified with creation. The same spirit entered people, notably the prophets, enabling them to speak and act for God. At his baptism by **John**, Jesus was specially equipped with the spirit, resulting in his remarkable public career (Acts 10.38). After his **resurrection**, his followers were themselves filled (Acts 2) by the same spirit, now identified as Jesus' own spirit: the creator God was acting afresh, remaking the world and them too. The spirit enabled them to live out a holiness which the **Torah** could not, producing 'fruit' in their lives, giving them 'gifts' with which to serve God, the world, and the church, and assuring them of future **resurrection** (Romans 8; Galatians 4—5; 1 Corinthians 12—14). From very early in Christianity (e.g. Galatians 4.1–7), the spirit became part of the new revolutionary definition of God himself: 'the one who sends the son and the spirit of the son'.

John (the Baptist)

Jesus' cousin on his mother's side, born a few months before Jesus; his father was a **priest**. He acted as a prophet, baptizing in the Jordan – dramatically re-enacting the Exodus from Egypt – to prepare people, by **repentance**, for God's coming judgment. He may have had some contact with the Essenes, though his eventual public message was different from theirs. Jesus' own vocation was decisively confirmed at his **baptism** by John. As part of John's message of the **kingdom**, he outspokenly criticized Herod Antipas for marrying his brother's wife. Herod had him imprisoned, and then beheaded him at his wife's request (Mark 6.14–29). Groups of John's disciples continued a separate existence, without merging into Christianity, for some time afterwards (e.g. Acts 19.1–7).

justification

God's declaration, from his position as judge of all the world, that someone is in the right, despite universal sin. This declaration will be made on the last day on the basis of an entire life (Romans 2.1–16), but is brought forward into the present on the basis of Jesus' achievement, because sin has been dealt with through his cross (Romans 3.21—4.25); the means of this present justification is simply **faith**. This means, particularly, that Jews and **Gentiles** alike are full members of the family promised by God to Abraham (Galatians 3; Romans 4).

kingdom of God, kingdom of heaven

Best understood as the king*ship*, or sovereign and saving rule, of Israel's God YHWH, as celebrated in several Psalms (e.g. 99.1) and prophecies (e.g. Daniel 6.26f.). Because YHWH was the creator God, when he finally became king in the way he intended this would involve setting the world to rights, and particularly rescuing Israel from its enemies. 'Kingdom of God' and various equivalents (e.g. 'No king but God!') became revolutionary slogans around the time of Jesus. Jesus' own announcement of God's kingdom redefined these expectations around his own very different plan and vocation. His invitation to people to 'enter' the kingdom was a way of summoning them to allegiance to himself and his programme, seen as the start of God's long-awaited saving reign. For Jesus, the kingdom was coming not in a single move, but in stages, of which his own public career was one, his death and resurrection another, and a still future consummation another. Note that 'kingdom of **heaven**' is Matthew's preferred form for the same phrase, following a regular Jewish practice of saying 'heaven' rather than 'God'. It does not refer to a place ('heaven'), but to the fact of God's becoming king in and through Jesus and his achievement. Paul speaks of Jesus, as **Messiah**, already in possession of his kingdom, waiting to hand it over finally to the Father (1 Corinthians 15.23–8; cf. Ephesians 5.5).

law, *see* **Torah**

life, spirit
Ancient people held many different views about what made human beings the special creatures they are. Some, including many Jews, believed that to be complete, humans needed bodies as well as inner selves. Others, including many influenced by the philosophy of Plato (fourth century BC), believed that the important part of a human was the 'soul' (Gk: *psyche*), which at death would be happily freed from its bodily prison. Confusingly for us, the same word *psyche* is often used in the New Testament within a Jewish framework where it clearly means 'life' or 'true self', without implying a body/soul dualism that devalues the body. Human inwardness of experience and understanding can also be referred to as 'spirit'. *See also* **holy spirit; resurrection**.

message, *see* **good news**

Messiah, Christ

The Hebrew word means literally 'anointed one', hence in theory either a prophet, **priest** or king. In Greek this translates as *Christos*; 'Christ' in early Christianity was a title, and only gradually became an alternative proper name for Jesus. In practice 'Messiah' is mostly restricted to the notion, which took various forms in ancient Judaism, of the coming king who would be David's true heir, through whom YHWH would rescue Israel from pagan enemies. There was no single template of expectations. Scriptural stories and promises contributed to different ideals and movements, often focused on (a) decisive military defeat of Israel's enemies and (b) rebuilding or cleansing the **Temple**. The **Dead Sea Scrolls** speak of two 'Messiahs', one a priest and the other a king. The universal early Christian belief that Jesus was Messiah is only explicable, granted his crucifixion by the Romans (which would have been seen as a clear sign that he was not the Messiah), by their belief that God had raised him from the dead, so vindicating the implicit messianic claims of his earlier ministry.

Mishnah

The main codification of Jewish law (**Torah**) by the **rabbis**, produced in about AD 200, reducing to writing the 'oral Torah' which in Jesus' day ran parallel to the 'written Torah'. The Mishnah is itself the basis of the much larger collections of traditions in the two Talmuds (roughly AD 400).

parousia

Literally, it means 'presence', as opposed to 'absence', and sometimes used by Paul with this sense (e.g. Philippians 2.12). It was already used in the Roman world for the ceremonial arrival of, for example, the emperor at a subject city or colony. Although the ascended Lord is not 'absent' from the church, when he 'appears' (Colossians 3.4; 1 John 3.2) in his 'second coming' this will be, in effect, an 'arrival' like that of the emperor, and Paul uses it thus in 1 Corinthians 15.23; 1 Thessalonians 2.19; etc. In the **gospels** it is found only in Matthew 24 (vv. 3, 27, 39).

Pharisees, lawyers

The Pharisees were an unofficial but powerful Jewish pressure group through most of the first centuries BC and AD. Largely lay-led, though including some priests, their aim was to purify Israel through intensified observance of the Jewish law (**Torah**), developing their own traditions about the precise meaning and application of scripture, their own patterns of prayer and other devotion, and their own calculations of the national hope. Though not all legal experts were Pharisees, most Pharisees were thus legal experts.

They effected a democratization of Israel's life, since for them the study and practice of Torah was equivalent to worshipping in the **Temple** – though they were adamant in pressing their own rules for the Temple liturgy on an unwilling (and often Sadducean) priesthood. This enabled them to survive AD 70 and, merging into the early Rabbinic movement, to develop new ways forward. Politically they stood up for ancestral traditions, and were at the forefront of various movements of revolt against both pagan overlordship and compromised Jewish leaders. By Jesus' day there were two distinct schools, the stricter one of Shammai, more inclined towards armed revolt, and the more lenient one of Hillel, ready to live and let live.

Jesus' debates with the Pharisees are at least as much a matter of agenda and policy (Jesus strongly opposed their separatist nationalism) as about details of theology and piety. Saul of Tarsus was a fervent right-wing Pharisee, presumably a Shammaite, until his conversion.

After the disastrous war of AD 66–70, these schools of Hillel and Shammai continued bitter debate on appropriate policy. Following the further disaster of AD 135 (the failed Bar-Kochba revolt against Rome) their traditions were carried on by the rabbis who, though looking to the earlier Pharisees for inspiration, developed a Torah-piety in which personal holiness and purity took the place of political agendas.

present age, age to come, eternal life

By the time of Jesus many Jewish thinkers divided history into two periods: 'the present age' and 'the age to come' – the latter being the time when YHWH would at last act decisively to judge evil, to rescue Israel, and to create a new world of justice and peace. The early

Christians believed that, though the full blessings of the coming age lay still in the future, it had already begun with Jesus, particularly with his death and **resurrection**, and that by **faith** and **baptism** they were able to enter it already. 'Eternal life' does not mean simply 'existence continuing without end', but 'the life of the age to come'.

priests, high priest

Aaron, the older brother of Moses, was appointed Israel's first high priest (Exodus 28—29), and in theory his descendents were Israel's priests thereafter. Other members of his tribe (Levi) were 'Levites', performing other liturgical duties but not sacrificing. Priests lived among the people all around the country, having a local teaching role (Leviticus 10.11; Malachi 2.7), and going to Jerusalem by rotation to perform the **Temple** liturgy (e.g. Luke 2.8).

David appointed Zadok (whose Aaronic ancestry is sometimes questioned) as high priest, and his family remained thereafter the senior priests in Jerusalem, probably the ancestors of the Sadducees. One explanation of the origins of the Qumran Essenes is that they were a dissident group who believed themselves to be the rightful chief priests.

rabbis, see Pharisees

repentance

Literally, this means 'turning back'. It is widely used in Old Testament and subsequent Jewish literature to indicate both a personal turning away from sin and Israel's corporate turning away from idolatry and back to YHWH. Through both meanings, it is linked to the idea of 'return from **exile**'; if Israel is to 'return' in all senses, it must 'return' to YHWH. This is at the heart of the summons of both **John the Baptist** and Jesus. In Paul's writings it is mostly used for **Gentiles** turning away from idols to serve the true God; also for sinning Christians who need to return to Jesus.

resurrection

In most biblical thought, human bodies matter and are not merely disposable prisons for the soul. When ancient Israelites wrestled with the goodness and justice of YHWH, the creator, they ultimately came to insist that he must raise the dead (Isaiah 26.19; Daniel 12.2–3) – a suggestion firmly resisted by classical pagan thought. The longed-for return from **exile** was also spoken of in terms of YHWH raising dry bones to new life (Ezekiel 37.1–14). These ideas were developed in the second-Temple period, not least at times of martyrdom (e.g. 2 Maccabees 7). Resurrection was not just 'life after death', but a newly embodied life *after* 'life after death'; those at present dead were either 'asleep', or seen as 'souls', 'angels' or 'spirits', awaiting new embodiment.

The early Christian belief that Jesus had been raised from the dead was not that he had 'gone to **heaven**', or that he had been 'exalted', or was 'divine'; they believed all those as well, but each could have been expressed without mention of resurrection. Only the bodily resurrection of Jesus explains the rise of the early church, particularly its belief in Jesus' messiahship (which his crucifixion would have called into question). The early Christians believed that they themselves would be raised to a new, transformed bodily life at the time of the Lord's return or **parousia** (e.g. Philippians 3.20f.).

sabbath

The Jewish sabbath, the seventh day of the week, was a regular reminder both of creation (Genesis 2.3; Exodus 20.8–11) and of the **Exodus** (Deuteronomy 5.15). Along with **circumcision** and the food laws, it was one of the badges of Jewish identity within the pagan world of late antiquity, and a considerable body of Jewish law and custom grew up around its observance.

sacrifice

Like all ancient people, the Israelites offered animal and vegetable sacrifices to their God. Unlike others, they possessed a highly detailed written code (mostly in Leviticus) for what to offer and how to offer it; this in turn was developed in the **Mishnah** (*c.* AD 200). The Old Testament specifies that sacrifices can only be offered in the Jerusalem **Temple**; after this was destroyed in AD 70, sacrifices ceased, and Judaism developed further the idea, already present in some teachings, of prayer, fasting and almsgiving as alternative forms of sacrifice. The early Christians used the language of sacrifice in connection with such things as holiness, evangelism and the **eucharist**.

the satan, demons

The Bible is never very precise about the identity of the figure known as 'the satan'. The Hebrew word means 'the accuser', and at times the satan seems to be a member of YHWH's heavenly council, with special responsibility as director of prosecutions (1 Chronicles 21.1; Job 1—2; Zechariah 3.1f.). However, it becomes identified variously with the serpent of the garden of Eden (Genesis 3.1–15) and with the rebellious daystar cast out of **heaven** (Isaiah 14.12–15), and was seen by many Jews as the quasi-personal source of evil standing behind both human wickedness and large-scale injustice, sometimes operating through semi-independent 'demons'. By Jesus' time various words were used to denote this figure, including Beelzebul/b (lit. 'Lord of the flies') and simply 'the evil one'; Jesus warned his followers against the deceits this figure could perpetrate. His opponents accused him of being in league with the satan, but the early Christians believed that Jesus in fact defeated it both in his own struggles with temptation (Matthew 4; Luke 4), his exorcisms of demons, and his death (1 Corinthians 2.8; Colossians 2.15). Final victory over this ultimate enemy is thus assured (Revelation 20), though the struggle can still be fierce for Christians (Ephesians 6.10–20).

son of God

Originally a title for Israel (Exodus 4.22) and the Davidic king (Psalm 2.7); also used of ancient angelic figures (Genesis 6.2). By the New Testament period it was already used as a **messianic** title, for example, in the **Dead Sea Scrolls**. There, and when used of Jesus in the gospels (e.g. Matthew 16.16), it means, or reinforces, 'Messiah', without the later significance of 'divine'. However, already in Paul the transition to the fuller meaning (one who was already equal with God and was sent by him to become human and to become Messiah) is apparent, without loss of the meaning 'Messiah' itself (e.g. Galatians 4.4).

son of man

In Hebrew or Aramaic, this simply means 'mortal', or 'human being'; in later Judaism, it is sometimes used to mean 'I' or 'someone like me'. In the New Testament the phrase is frequently linked to

Daniel 7.13, where 'one like a son of man' is brought on the clouds of **heaven** to 'the Ancient of Days', being vindicated after a period of suffering, and is given kingly power. Though Daniel 7 itself interprets this as code for 'the people of the saints of the Most High', by the first century some Jews understood it as a **messianic** promise. Jesus developed this in his own way in certain key sayings which are best understood as promises that God would vindicate him, and judge those who had opposed him, after his own suffering (e.g. Mark 14.62). Jesus was thus able to use the phrase as a cryptic self-designation, hinting at his coming suffering, his vindication, and his God-given authority.

spirit, *see* **life, holy spirit**

Temple

The Temple in Jerusalem was planned by David (*c.* 1000 BC) and built by his son Solomon as the central sanctuary for all Israel. After reforms under Hezekiah and Josiah in the seventh century BC, it was destroyed by Babylon in 587 BC. Rebuilding by the returned **exiles** began in 538 BC, and was completed in 516, initiating the 'second-Temple period'. Judas Maccabaeus cleansed it in 164 BC after its desecration by Antiochus Epiphanes (167). Herod the Great began to rebuild and beautify it in 19 BC; the work was completed in AD 63. The Temple was destroyed by the Romans in AD 70. Many Jews believed it should and would be rebuilt; some still do. The Temple was not only the place of **sacrifice**; it was believed to be the unique dwelling of YHWH on earth, the place where **heaven** and earth met.

Torah, law

'Torah', narrowly conceived, consists of the first five books of the Old Testament, the 'five books of Moses' or 'Pentateuch'. (These contain much law, but also much narrative.) It can also be used for the whole Old Testament scriptures, though strictly these are the 'Law, prophets and writings'. In a broader sense, it refers to the whole developing corpus of Jewish legal tradition, written and oral; the oral Torah was initially codified in the **Mishnah** around AD 200, with wider developments found in the two Talmuds, of Babylon and Jerusalem, codified around AD 400. Many Jews in the time of Jesus and Paul regarded the Torah as being so strongly God-given as to be almost itself, in some sense, divine; some (e.g. Ben-Sirach 24) identified it with the figure of 'Wisdom'. Doing what Torah said was not seen as a means of earning God's favour, but rather of expressing gratitude, and as a key badge of Jewish identity.

Word, *see* **good news**

YHWH

The ancient Israelite name for God, from at least the time of the **Exodus** (Exodus 6.2f.). It may originally have been pronounced 'Yahweh', but by the time of Jesus it was considered too holy to speak out loud, except for the **high priest** once a year in the Holy of Holies in the **Temple**. Instead, when reading scripture, pious Jews would say *Adonai*, 'Lord', marking this usage by adding the vowels of *Adonai* to the consonants of YHWH, eventually producing the hybrid 'Jehovah'. The word YHWH is formed from the verb 'to be', combining 'I am who I am', 'I will be who I will be', and perhaps 'I am because I am', emphasizing YHWH's sovereign creative power.